accounting. Worked ᵃ   ͏ᵗᵒ the number on the
the exposition, and exercises (wiu.   ͏͏ ͏required.
are also chapters on the interpretation of acc͏.
for price changes, and on broader aspects of acc͏
emphasis throughout is on understanding fundamental prin͏ᵢₚᵢₑs
rather than on detailed practical procedures.

The book is primarily addressed to university students who are
meeting the subject for the first time, and is also a first introduction
for students preparing for professional examinations, giving them
a grounding in the fundamental nature of accounting which is lost
in other more compendious introductory texts.

———

GEOFFREY WHITTINGTON is Price Waterhouse Professor
of Financial Accounting at the University of Cambridge, and a
Fellow of Fitzwilliam College. He was previously Professor at the
University of Edinburgh and then the University of Bristol, where
he was also head of the Department of Economics and Dean of the
Social Science Faculty. He is currently a part-time member of the
Monopolies and Mergers Commission, and Academic Adviser to
the Accounting Standards Board. He is the author of four other
books (all with Cambridge) including *Inflation Accounting: An
Introduction to the Debate*, and over fifty papers in academic and
professional publications.

THE ELEMENTS OF
ACCOUNTING

THE ELEMENTS OF
ACCOUNTING

AN INTRODUCTION

GEOFFREY WHITTINGTON

CAMBRIDGE
UNIVERSITY PRESS

Published by the Press Syndicate of the University of Cambridge
The Pitt Building, Trumpington Street, Cambridge CB2 1RP
40 West 20th Street, New York, NY 10011–4211, USA
10 Stamford Road, Oakleigh, Melbourne 3166, Australia

First published 1992
Reprinted 1996, 1997

A catalogue record for this book is available from the British Library

Library of Congress cataloguing in publication data applied for

ISBN 0 521 41392 3 hardback
ISBN 0 521 42449 6 paperback

Transferred to digital printing 1999

CE

To Barbara, Debbie and Val

CONTENTS

PREFACE

ORIGINS

In 1972, when I was appointed to the Chair of Accountancy and Finance at Edinburgh University, I had never given a lecture on accounting. I was faced immediately by a group of more than a hundred first-year undergraduates, fresh from school and keen to learn about accounting to advance their careers, typically with the aim of becoming Scottish Chartered Accountants. What was I to tell them? I had a horror of the then typical compendious introductory text-book (and still quite common) which recited detailed book-keeping routines in an apparently aimless manner, with no logical foundation. On the other hand, I was convinced that in order to study accounting it was necessary to be able to *do* accounting, at least to the extent of preparing a set of basic financial statements for a simple business. I therefore resolved to explain the essential logic of the accounting framework, using numerical illustrations, but emphasising principles rather than the fine detail of practice. My attitude to the subject had been shaped by my first teachers at the London School of Economics, Professor William Baxter and Professor Harold Edey, and it was to Professor Edey's *Introduction to Accounting* that I turned as the recommended text. The influence of Prof. Edey's book is still apparent in my current introductory teaching, as reflected in this book.

After leaving Edinburgh, I taught introductory accounting to a large first-year economics and accounting group at Bristol, and later, in Cambridge, I introduced the subject to Part I Economics Tripos students at Cambridge. Each of these audiences had made different demands and has led me to adjust the exposition, but the central theme has remained the same. The present book is an attempt to state that theme in a more permanent and, hopefully, more orderly manner. The intended audience is any intelligent student who is approaching accounting for the first time, either in university or in professional studies. The level of the book is elementary and it is aimed at the non-specialist as much as the intending specialist. It is hoped that most readers will be persuaded to take their studies further: contrary to its popular image, accounting is an interesting subject as well as an important one.

PLAN OF THE BOOK

Chapter 1 introduces some necessary foundation material. It describes some fundamental assumptions used in constructing accounts and gives a simple numerical illustration of some basic accounting statements. Some of the material in this chapter may seem difficult to a beginner, but it should become clearer after reading later chapters. This chapter provides some necessary warnings which any beginner in the field should have in mind, even if they are not fully appreciated at first reading, and it may be worthwhile to re-read chapter 1 after finishing the rest of the book.

Chapters 2 and 5 form the heart of the book. They explore the logic of double entry accounting, starting from the balance sheet identity and deriving from this the profit and loss account, the flow of funds statement, and the accounting system which is used to store the information from which these statements are prepared. The techniques explained in these chapters are at the heart of accounting and provide the key to many of the arcane rituals with which accountants often impress or confuse non-accountants.

Chapter 6 turns to the use of accounts. In particular, it discusses the interpretation of the summary financial statements which are prepared by businesses. Chapter 7 extends this theme by explaining the elements of accounting for changing prices. Price changes pose particularly important problems for the interpretation and usefulness of accounts which are prepared on the historical cost convention. Furthermore, the techniques of price change accounting provide an opportunity to gain further insights into the fundamental accounting relationships described in chapters 2 and 5.

Chapter 8 provides an important diversion. It looks behind the information used in earlier chapters to illustrate the preparation of financial statements and considers how such information is collected and recorded. In practice accurate collection and recording are essential aspects of good accounting and occupy much of the attention of accountants and the auditors who check their work.

Finally, chapter 9 outlines some of the aspects of accounting which are necessarily excluded from full treatment in an elementary introduction. This chapter also contains suggestions for further reading. It is hoped that most readers will eventually find their way to chapter 9 and that they will still have sufficient enthusiasm to read further. Accounting is now a veritable Aladdin's cave of interesting ideas and good reading. This is in stark contrast with the situation thirty-five years ago, when the present author first studied accounting. In those days, the subject seemed to be a very primitive cave, inhabited largely by intellectual cave men who rehearsed apparently meaningless rituals for professional examinations.

ACKNOWLEDGEMENTS

It is a great pleasure to acknowledge the support of those who have made the writing of this book possible, despite the fact that the end product may not do it justice.

The first acknowledgement must be to Price Waterhouse, who founded the Chair of Financial Accounting at Cambridge which I held whilst writing this book. The book and the individual may not do them particular credit, but it is surely most creditable to have founded the first chair of financial accounting in either of the two senior English universities.

The second acknowledgement is the intellectual debt to all those who have contributed ideas or criticism which are reflected in the text, although the usual disclaimer applies: they are not responsible for the errors or inadequacies of the book. The debt to Professors Baxter and Edey has already been acknowledged. Numerous others have made contributions which are difficult to identify and impossible to acknowledge fully. Amongst these are the mainly anonymous referees who read earlier drafts for Cambridge University Press. One of these who is identifiable is Professor Ken Peasnell, of the University of Lancaster, who devoted more time than the manuscript deserved to correcting errors of exposition and suggesting improvements. David Tweedie, my collaborator in several publications, allowed me to use his 'tennis court' exercise (chapter 6), and my other illustrations and examples owe their origins to the methods (although not the exact form) devised by other teachers of the subject. I also received some useful critical comments, from the standpoint of the intended reader (a beginner in the subject) from my wife, Joyce, and my elder son, Alan. They both gave up at the end of chapter 5, but I like to think that this was due to lack of time rather than lack of interest.

Finally, the whole typescript was prepared under great pressure, and with equally great patience and skill, by my secretary, Barbara Brewer. Since I moved to Edinburgh in 1972, I have had only three secretaries, Debbie Hathorn in Edinburgh (1972–5), Val Harvey in Bristol (1975–88) and Barbara Brewer in Cambridge (since 1988). They have all, in their different ways, given me the high level of support which I needed but probably did not deserve. For this reason, this book is dedicated to them.

Geoffrey Whittington
Cambridge, January 1991

Chapter 1

BASIC CONCEPTS

INTRODUCTION

This book is intended to introduce an absolute beginner to the basic elements of accounting. It deals with what might be called the 'hard core' of accounting. It is the core because the logical structure of the basic accounting statements and the underlying concepts of double entry book-keeping are the heart of what is unique to accounting as a technique and a discipline: for the rest, accounting is an eclectic subject, using relevant parts of many other disciplines, ranging from economics and statistics to law and social psychology. It is appropriate to describe it as the *hard* core for two reasons. Firstly, it is rigorous and logical. Secondly, it is often difficult to learn, mainly because it is usually very badly explained. This book is intended to remedy the latter problem, but many others have attempted this task and failed, so that there is no standard introductory text on the subject which commands universal respect: a more realistic ambition might therefore be to explain the subject a little more clearly than is done elsewhere.

It is a pity that the basic elements of accounting are not more widely understood, because they offer essential insights into the way in which economic activity is measured, and hence the way in which economic decisions are made. Everyone is engaged in economic activity, whether it be in the affairs of a small club (usually managed on the basis of cash flow accounts, of varying degrees of eccentricity), or in the economic fortunes of the nation (usually measured by means of national income accounts, which are notorious for measurement errors, despite the reverence in which their 'bottom line' measure of Gross National Product (GNP) is held). Thus, everyone has contact with some form of accounting data, and most people are confused and misled by them. This explains the power and importance of accountants in our society: their ability to represent and interpret financial information gives them considerable influence over decisions. This does not mean that

1

accountants always understand as much as they believe or pretend to believe. They are almost unique among the professions (or at least those which claim to be learned professions) in their widespread contempt for the study of the subject matter of their profession; the consequences of this were seen in their confusion over price change accounting, when this became an issue in the 1970s and 1980s. However, accountants do usually understand their accounts better than the general public, and this gives them power and prosperity.

TYPES OF ACCOUNTING INFORMATION: FINANCIAL ACCOUNTING AND MANAGEMENT ACCOUNTING

All accounting is concerned with providing information relating to economic activity. There is a great variety of economic activities and of types of information relating to those activities. It would be confusing to introduce all of this variety at an early stage: we shall instead concentrate on the basic elements of the accounting framework using one particular (but very common) type of information. However, it is important, even at this early stage, to have a broad awareness of the variety of accounting information, and so, for illustrative purposes, we shall consider the broad distinction which is often made between management accounting and financial accounting. This distinction is akin to that often made in economics between macro and micro economics: both can be used to provide a convenient taxonomy of their respective subjects, but neither dichotomy is perfect, there being important underlying common elements.

Management accounting is concerned with the provision of information to the management of an accounting entity, typically a company or firm, but sometimes a group of companies or a division of a company. It is therefore internal information for use only within the organisation and is oriented towards the needs of its managers. These needs will include information to aid current control of the organisations activities and decision-making which will have future consequences. Thus, management information will have a strong bias towards the present and the future, although *ex post* appraisal of past performance will also play a part. Future information is typically embodied in budgets, and budgeting is an important aspect of management accounting at all levels, from the individual to the nation. Management accounting is adapted to the particular needs of management and so is likely to vary a great deal between organisations, depending on their needs and management styles, and it is not regulated or standardised by any external agency. This subject is discussed further, albeit briefly, in chapter 9.

Financial accounting, on the other hand, is directed mainly to providers of finance, i.e., shareholders and creditors, who are external to the organisation. In recent years, there has also been a greater emphasis on other potential external users of financial accounts, such as suppliers, customers and the general public. The external nature of users of financial accounts has led to three characteristics of conventional financial accounts. Firstly, they are oriented towards *ex post* evaluation of past performance (sometimes described as 'stewardship') rather than with the potential consequences of current and future decisions, which concern management. Secondly, there is a preference for information which is objective, providing a reliable check on managers. This is typically reinforced by checking or 'audit' of the accounts by independent firms of auditors (the majority of whom are, somewhat confusingly, described as chartered accountants: an accountant prepares the accounts, whereas an auditor checks them). Thirdly, the form and content of financial accounts, unlike management accounts, is typically regulated by external bodies, in order to ensure comparability between firms and to ensure that management does not exploit its monopoly of information to the disadvantage of shareholders and others. In the UK currently, financial accounts are regulated by the Companies Acts (in the case of companies) and other legislation (e.g., the Building Societies Act). This regulation is extended by the Accounting Standards Board which has legal authority derived from the 1989 Companies Act, and extended further, in the case of companies whose shares are listed on the stock exchange, by the listing requirements of the stock exchange. For the purposes of this book, we shall confine our discussion to profit-oriented businesses. However, the reader should be aware that not-for-profit organisations, such as charities, have special information requirements which change the appropriate form of the financial accounts, although the underlying logic of double-entry accounting still applies.

Thus, the broad orientation of management accounting is towards the present and future, and, therefore, to 'softer', less reliable information. Financial accounting, on the other hand, has traditionally concentrated more on the evaluation of past performance and on 'harder', more reliable evidence. However, this is mainly a matter of emphasis rather than fundamental difference. The data base, relating to the transactions and to the assets and liabilities of the firm (we shall use this term rather than the more accurate but more cumbersome 'accounting entity'), is common to both management and financial accounting systems, as is the basic framework of accounting. Moreover, as investors and financial markets become more sophisticated, there are pressures for financial accounting to adopt more of the future orientation of management accounting (e.g., see *Making Corporate Reports Valuable*, The Institute of Chartered Accountants of Scotland, 1988).

For the sake of simplicity, we shall concentrate on financial accounting, illustrating its framework by applying the traditional methods of historical cost accounting. This is the most common form of accounting encountered by most people in practice, but it is important not to be seduced by its apparent objectivity and plausibility. We shall therefore explain its basic assumptions before launching into numerical examples. Later, in chapter 7, we shall demonstrate how alternative methods, recording changing prices, can be accommodated within the accounting framework.

THE CONVENTIONS OF TRADITIONAL FINANCIAL ACCOUNTING

As explained above, financial accounting is intended for users external to the firm and has therefore traditionally concentrated on 'hard' *objective* information, suitable for checking by auditors. There has also evolved a practice of exercising *prudence* (sometimes referred to as conservatism), i.e., to over-state liabilities and under-state assets where there is a choice of valuations. The object of this is the protection of creditors and other users of accounts who might otherwise be misled by management's choice of optimistic values of the assets (and under-statement of liabilities) of the firm. Another practice which is regarded as highly desirable in traditional accounting practice (and, like prudence, is part of current UK standard accounting practice) is *consistency*. This requires that the same accounting policies be followed through time, so that year-to-year comparison of a firm's performance is not confused by changes of accounting method.

The traditional model of financial accounting, which embodies these properties of objectivity, prudence and consistency is based on *historical cost* (HC), i.e., assets are valued at what they were bought for rather than what they are worth now. This has the advantage of being relatively objective: it is much easier to check what an asset actually cost than to assess what it *might* cost or be sold for now or in the future. If HC is adhered to from year to year, it should also lead to a degree of consistency (subject to some reservations). However, the HC principle does not guarantee prudence because market values can fall as well as rise. Thus, an asset may be worth less than was paid for it. In such cases, the strict HC principle is often modified by the rule 'cost or market value, whichever is the lower': this is standard practice for current assets (those likely to be realised within the immediate future in the ordinary course of business) in the UK. The HC valuation rule has also been modified in the UK and elsewhere by the demands of *relevance*: it is possible to mislead a user of accounts by producing information which (like HC) is objective, but which does not reflect current economic reality[1] when prices have changed. Thus, in the case of durable assets which have a ready market (such as marketable securities and real property held as an investment), revaluations are common and are in some cases required by law.

Apart from these breaches of the HC system to introduce current values in the cause of prudence or relevance, HC itself is not as easy to implement or as objective as it might seem. If we try to measure profit on an HC basis, we recognise revenue on the basis of the *realisation* principle, i.e., a sales transaction is necessary before we recognise a gain in value of an asset over its historical cost. This is a simple idea if we are engaged in the purchase and sale of a commodity (which we shall call a standard widget) for cash, with no processing by the firm: in such a case, widgets are valued at what they cost (HC) until they are sold (when selling price is substituted and a profit arises). However, suppose we are not selling widgets, but are instead engaged on long-term contract work, such as building the Channel Tunnel. In such a case, it would appear misleading to recognise no profit (if there is any) before the project is complete, and accountants usually relax their strict realisation rule to allow some profit to be recognised as stages of the project are completed. There are other cases when the point of realisation is less than clear, for legal reasons, e.g., when there are options to return goods to the supplier.

The problems of calculating profit on a 'pure' HC basis are by no means confined to the assessment of revenue. Costs are at least as difficult to measure on a HC basis. For example, not all of the outlays of a period are related to revenues earned in the period: others may be incurred for future benefit, or be final payments related to a past benefit. Accountants have tried to overcome this problem by adopting the *matching* principle, i.e., in calculating the profits of a period, they try to match costs to revenues by charging only those costs relating to revenues earned in the period. This may lead to some outlays of a period being treated not as costs of the period but as assets, giving rise to future benefit, e.g., prepaid rent or insurance premiums. The most obvious outlay of this type is a 'fixed asset', which is expected to give benefit over several future periods and is 'written off' gradually over those periods by means of a charge for depreciation (as explained in chapter 5).

All of these techniques will be illustrated later. For the present, it is sufficient to be aware that they introduce a significant degree of *subjectivity* into the apparently objective 'pure' HC system, by posing such questions as 'How much of this contract should we regard as being completed in this period?' or 'What proportion of this asset should be regarded as used up in depreciation during the period?'. Nevertheless, HC is the traditional method of accounting and, despite its complexities, it is easier to understand than some of the alternatives, which may explain its persisting popularity. We shall therefore use it in our basic illustrations of the accounting system. The purpose of this initial discussion has been to warn the reader not to believe that the results of using HC always provide an objective, accurate or relevant picture of the current economic state of the firm. Later (chapter 7), we shall see how the accounting system can be based on current prices rather than HC. Many writers on the subject, and some practising accountants, believe that current prices give a better picture of the current economic condition of a business.

CASH FLOW AND ACCRUAL ACCOUNTING

Perhaps the most intuitively satisfying and most objective form of accounting is not historical cost accounting but cash flow accounting. Why not simply record the cash receipts and payments of a period, without the complications of the realisation or matching principles? Such a statement might be as follows:

Cash flow for the year ended 31 December

	£	£
Opening cash balance, 1 January		100
Receipts during the year	2,000	
Less payments during the year	1,500	
Net receipts for the year		500
Closing cash balance, 31 December		600

This statement scores well on objectivity: it can easily be checked by counting the cash[2] or, if (as would often be the case in a business) the cash transactions are carried out through a bank, by checking the bank statements. The cash flow system can also claim relevance, in that cash flows are a crucial ingredient in the economist's concept of present value (PV) which is based on expected future cash flows adjusted ('discounted') for the effects of timing.[3] These features have attracted a number of academic writers on accounting to advocate cash flow as a basis of financial reporting. Nevertheless, the idea has not caught on in practice. The reason is very simple: present value calculations are based on cash flows over the complete lifetime of an investment, whereas financial reports deal with a short period (usually a year or part of a year), rather than the whole life. Moreover firms, with which financial reports are typically concerned, may be expected to continue in existence over an indefinite future. Thus, to provide a complete evaluation of a continuing firm, we would need projected cash flows for all future years of a firm's existence, as well as a series of past cash flows. This would not only involve processing a large amount of data, but also the estimation of future flows would destroy the pure objectivity of this type of information.

The accountant's traditional response to the difficulty of reporting the performance of a firm over an individual year has been *accrual accounting*, of which historical cost accounting is one example. Accrual accounting attempts to allocate revenues to the periods in which they were earned and costs to the periods in which they were incurred, rather than allocating revenues and costs to the time period in which the cash receipts of payments occurred. To illustrate how this works, let us assume the following additional facts about the firm described in our cash flow example:

(1) At the end of the year the firm owed its creditors £100.
(2) At the end of the year the firm's debtors owed it £200.
(3) At the end of the year the firm held stock which had cost £200.

For simplicity, we assume that the only initial asset or liability was £100 in cash (perhaps because the business was started at the beginning of the year), so that there is no need to adjust for opening assets and liabilities.

Accrual accounting is based, in this case, on the following calculation:

(1) Cash receipts are converted into sales, as follows:

	£
Cash receipts	2,000
Add amounts due from debtors	200
Total sales	2,200

This is an application of the realisation principle: the debtors had legally bought the goods, so that a sale is recognised, although the payment is not yet made.

(2) Cash payments are converted into cost of sales, as follows:

	£
Cash payments	1,500
Add amount due to creditors	100
	1,600
Less amount paid for stock not sold at end of year	200
Cost of goods sold	1,400

This is an application of the matching principle. The stocks were held for future benefit, so that their cost is not charged against sales of this period. Until they are sold, they are an asset rather than cost to the business.

We now have a profit statement, commonly called a profit and loss account:

Profit and loss account
for the year ended 31 December

	£
Sales	2,200
Less cost of sales	1,400
Profit for the year	800

The profit (£800) is, in this case, much larger than the net cash receipts (£500). The difference (£300) represents the increase in net assets other than cash (stocks £200, plus debtors £200, less creditors £100). This draws attention to the subjective nature of profit measurement: other methods of valuing stocks (e.g., current value rather than historical cost) or debtors (e.g., applying a discount factor to allow for lost interest if payment were likely to be received at a significantly distant date in the future, or applying a 'bad debts' provision if the debts were not likely to be repaid in full) would lead to different measures of profit.

The relationship of profit measurement to asset valuation is best seen by looking at another financial statement, the *balance sheet*. This shows the assets and liabilities of the firm, with the proprietor's interest in the business as the residual. At the beginning of the year, the balance sheet was very simple, with one asset (cash) owned by the proprietor:

Balance sheet
as at 1 January

	£		£
Proprietor's capital	100	Cash	100

At the end of the year, the balance sheet includes the assets and liabilities which have arisen:

Balance sheet
as at 31 December

Proprietor's capital	£	Current assets	£
Opening balance, 1 January	100	Stocks	200
Add profit for the year	800	Debtors	200
	900	Cash	600
Current liabilities			
Creditors	100		
	1,000		1,000

The assets listed on the right-hand side are all called current assets, because they are retained for immediate use in the business and are unlikely to be held for very long (for, say, longer than twelve months). They sum to £1,000. Deducting the liabilities (described as current because they are due for payment in the near future) of £100 leaves net assets of £900. This is the amount of the proprietor's capital, made up of an opening balance of £100 and profit for the period of £800. It is no accident that adding profit in this way gives a value of proprietor's capital which just balances the balance sheet: the profit calculation presented earlier was based on changes of all of the assets and liabilities which make up the net assets figure in the balance sheet. This relationship between profit and the change in net assets is often described as *articulation* of the profit and loss account with the balance sheet. It is the reason why asset (and liability) measurement conventions affect the profit figure: they are part of the calculation of profit. Articulation is a logical feature of the accounting system, but it is sometimes found inconvenient by those who do not like all asset value changes to affect profit. To avoid this problem, cunning accountants have devised systems of reserve accounting, which obscure the underlying relationship. Such systems are at the heart of many 'cosmetic accounting' schemes, designed to dress up the accounts to look more pleasing to users, although the motives for reserve accounting are not always so base. However, these problems are of a more sophisticated type than need worry us here. For the moment, we shall deal with fully articulated accounts, in order to understand the fundamental relationship between profit calculation and the balance sheet.

In order to complete our picture of the performance of this very simple firm, it is necessary to introduce one further financial statement, the *flow of funds statement*. This shows how the balance sheet has changed during the period, and its raw material is obtained by deducting the opening value of each item in the balance sheet from the closing value. An increase in an item on the left-hand side of the balance sheet (or a decrease in a right-hand item) will be described as a source of funds and an increase in an item on the right-hand side (or a decrease in a left-hand item) will be described as a use of funds. The relevant changes in our particular example are:

		£
Sources:	proprietor's capital (profit for the period)	800
	increase in creditors	100
Uses:	increase in stocks	200
	increase in debtors	200
	increase in cash	500

We can formally arrange this as a flow of funds statement in two alternative ways. Firstly, we can treat cash as the residual:

Flow of funds statement
for the year ended 31 December

Sources	£	£
Profit for the period	800	
Increase in creditors	100	
Less: uses		900
Increase in stocks	200	
Increase in debtors	200	
		400
Change in cash balance		500

This has the unfortunate possibility that it will lend credence to the popular misapprehension that a *funds* flow statement is a *cash* flow statement. In fact, a cash flow statement should, like that given earlier, be composed entirely of cash flows, not of funds flows which are calculated on an accruals basis (as is the case here).

This problem is overcome by the second format, which treats the whole of working capital (stocks, cash and debtors less creditors) as the residual item. In the present case, there are no uses (such as investment in fixed assets) other than changes in working capital, so a suitable format might be:

**Flow of funds statement
for the year ended 31 December**

	£
Source of funds	
Profit for the period	800
Use of funds	
Change in working capital*	800

(*Stocks 200, debtors 200, cash 500, creditors 100).

RETROSPECT

In this chapter, we defined accounting as the provision of information relating to economic activity. We considered various types and uses of accounting information. The subsequent exposition will concentrate on the framework of *financial accounting* (addressed to users external to the firm) rather than management accounting (addressed to users internal to the firm) and will use the *historical cost* convention for illustrative purposes, although the limitations of that convention were explained. Finally, *cash flow* accounting was explained and illustrated as was, by contrast, *accrual accounting* using the historical cost convention. The numerical illustrations also introduced *three basic financial statements*: the profit and loss account, the balance sheet and the flow of funds statement. Chapter 2 explains this basic framework in more detail.

Chapter 2

THE ACCOUNTING FRAMEWORK

INTRODUCTION

At the end of the previous chapter, we considered a simple numerical example of a business and used this to illustrate three basic financial statements, which summarise the economic activity of the firm during a period, within the framework of accrual accounting. These were the balance sheet, the profit and loss account, and the flow of funds statement. In this chapter, we shall explore the accounting framework with two objectives. Firstly, we need to understand how transactions can be recorded and ordered systematically in order to prepare the summary statements: the way in which our numerical example was constructed was informal and would have been cumbersome to use if there had been more transactions. Secondly, in understanding how the statements are constructed from individual transactions, we hope to understand more about the properties of the statements and the relationship between them.

THE BALANCE SHEET

The balance sheet is the fundamental accounting statement. This does not necessarily mean that it is the most important statement: that is a matter for users of accounts and many would prefer the profit and loss account if they were allowed to see only one statement. However, the balance sheet is fundamental in that it expresses the basic identity which underlies all double entry accounting.

In the previous chapter, we saw that the balance sheet contained a list of assets on one side (the right-hand side in the UK: the left-hand side in the USA) and liabilities on the other side, together with the proprietor's capital, which provided the balancing item. A formal definition of the balance sheet might be that it is *a statement of assets and claims at a point in time*. Note that the term 'claims' is used, rather than

13

'liabilities'. Claims include all types of claim on the business, including the proprietor's claim to the ownership of any residual net asset or 'net worth' (which is why the proprietor can claim profits and bears losses): this is often referred to as an 'equity' interest and in companies is represented by the ordinary shareholders' claim. The liabilities are a different type of claim, representing the right to claim a fixed sum. It should also be noted that the definition of the balance sheet refers to a point in time: it is a snapshot picture of the firm, recording, in economist's terms, stocks at a point in time rather than flows through time. It is also rather important to remember that the assets and claims should be measured at the *same* point in time if the balance sheet is to have its proper meaning, and if it is to be guaranteed to balance!

Because the balance sheet is fundamental to all that follows, it is worth stating its properties in a more formal manner.

The *components* of the balance sheet are as follows:

Component	Algebraic notation (subscripts imply a point in time)	Conventional subdivisions
Assets	A_t	Fixed
		Current
Liabilities	L_t	Long-term
		Short-term
Net worth	N_t	Capital contributed by proprietors*
		Retained profits

Note: * Ordinary shareholders, in a company.

The *relationship* between the components, or balance sheet equation, is as follows:

$$A_t = L_t + N_t$$

where the left-hand side of the equation refers to the right-hand side of the balance sheet as illustrated in chapter 1.

This relationship always holds unless there is an error in recording or processing, i.e., *the balance sheet always balances*. It is therefore a sign of complete ignorance of the elements of accounting to talk about 'making the balance sheet balance', as if this was a problem of financial management rather than arithmetic. The relationship is, in fact, an *identity* rather than an equation, because it arises from the definition of the proprietor's equity interest:

$$N_t \equiv A_t - L_t$$

The nature of that interest is that the proprietor owns the residual, whether it includes a profit or a loss, thus balancing the balance sheet. Essentially, the identity arises from our society's rule that every asset must have an owner: thus, all the assets in a business, after deducting creditors' claims, accrue to the owner (proprietor) of the business.

Having propounded the strong arithmetic rule, that the balance sheet always balances, it is important to remember that arithmetic consistency does not imply economic significance. Although we refer to N_t as 'net worth', it does not necessarily equal what the proprietor's interest is worth in the market place: hence it would be most unusual for a company's net assets per share to equal the market price of a share as determined by the stock market. This is partly because of the unrealistic asset valuations resulting from using the historical cost convention, but it is also due to the fact that the market value of a business as a going concern is often greater than the market value of the sum of the individual assets, the difference being descibed as goodwill.[1]

AN ILLUSTRATION OF THE BALANCE SHEET

Before embarking on a deeper exploration of the accounting system and how it works, it is important to understand some of the formal details of balance sheets, as they are conventionally drawn up. Example 2.1 provides an illustration, based broadly on current accounting practice, but not conforming precisely to the requirements of the Companies Acts or other statutory requirements, which will vary according to the nature and status of the accounting entity (which we loosely refer to as a firm).

Example 2.1   The balance sheet

Horizontal format

Sidgwick industries
Balance sheet
as at *30 September 19..*

	£		£	£
Capital		*Fixed assets*		
Capital subscribed by proprietors	50,000	Freehold premises		50,000
		Plant and machinery:		
Plus accumulated profits	35,000	cost	30,000	
		Less depreciation	10,000	
	85,000			20,000
		Motor vehicles: cost	20,000	
		Less depreciation	10,000	
				10,000
				80,000
Long-term liability (due after more than one year)		Long-term investments		24,000
				104,900
Loan, secured by a mortgage on freehold property	20,000			
		Current assets		
		Stock and work-in-progress	10,000	
Current liabilities		Trade debtors and prepayments	15,000	
Trade creditors and accrued charges	15,000	Cash	100	
Bank overdraft	10,000			
	25,000			25,100
	£ 130,000			£ 130,000

Vertical format

Sidgwick industries
Balance sheet
as at *30 September 19..*

		£	£
ASSETS EMPLOYED:			
Fixed assets			
Freehold premises			50,000
plant and machinery:	cost	30,000	
	Less depreciation	10,000	
			20,000
Motor vehicles:	cost	20,000	
	Less depreciation	10,000	
			10,000
			80,000
Long-term investments			24,900
			104,900
Current assets			
Stock and work-in-progress		10,000	
Trade debtors and prepayments		15,000	
Cash		100	
		25,100	
Less: current liabilities			
Trade creditors and accrued charges		15,000	
Bank overdraft		10,000	
		25,000	
Net current assets			100
			£105,000
FINANCED BY:			
Long-term liability (due after more than one year)			
Loan, secured by a mortgage on freehold property			20,000
Capital			
Capital subscribed by proprietors		50,000	
Plus accumulated profits		35,000	
			85,000
			£105,000

The first thing to note about example 2.1 is that it offers the balance sheet in two alternative formats. The first is the conventional horizontal format, used in the illustration in chapter 1. This lists the assets on one side and the claims on the other. Its advantage is that it clearly shows the working of the balance sheet equation. It also conforms with the format of traditional ledger accounts (which will be illustrated in later chapters), which is why it is the traditional method of presenting a balance sheet. The alternative format, illustrated second, is the vertical format. This is more of a narrative form and can be read down the page like a book. It usually starts by listing and summing the fixed and current assets and listing, summing and deducting the current liabilities. It thus arrives at a total for the net assets requiring long-term finance, either proprietors' equity or long-term loans. This finance is listed and summed in the final section, the sum equalling the sum of the assets requiring finance, so that the balance sheet equation holds. This format is currently the more popular for presenting the balance sheets of large public companies, because there is a belief that it is more easily comprehended by the casual or non-expert reader.

The detail is the same in both formats. It is worth noting the convention that assets and liabilities are usually listed in order of their liquidity, i.e., the length of the period before they are converted into cash receipts or payments. Thus, fixed assets are listed before current assets and, within these categories, the most permanent assets are listed first, e.g., stocks are listed before debtors and cash is listed last. On the claims side of the horizontal format, the proprietors' equity capital is listed first (because it will remain in the business for an indefinite period), long-term liabilities, which are repayable in the relatively distant future, are listed next, and short-term 'current' liabilities are listed last. The vertical format slightly disturbs this sequence for the claims side by putting long-term financing at the bottom of the statement.

The detailed items give a sample of some of the more common items appearing in balance sheets. The capital subscribed by the proprietors is not described as shares, so we may assume that this is an unincorporated business (i.e., not a company). The long-term liability (defined conventionally as one due more than a year after the balance sheet date) is secured by a mortgage: in a company, a common legal charge of this type is called a debenture, and loans protected by it are often referred to as 'debentures' (the legal charge gives the lenders the right to sell a particular asset or groups of assets to repay the loan, or interest on it, should the company fail to do so). These loans usually have interest payments attached to them. Trade creditors are an important current liability in most businesses: they represent amounts owed by the company to suppliers who have not yet been paid. Accrued charges include expenses which have accumulated (e.g., rent or electricity charges) for which a bill has not yet been rendered by the supplier (the 'creditor').

On the assets side, the fixed assets have been recorded at cost, although many firms now revalue them from time to time, and depreciation has been deducted from all of the assets which have a finite life (this is generally accepted practice in the UK). The depreciation reflects the proportion of assets' potential services which have been used up. Stock is the raw materials or finished goods held by the business and work-in-progress represents part-finished products. The latter can be difficult to value with precision, even within the historical cost convention. Trade debtors are the mirror image of trade creditors: they are customers who have not yet paid for goods or services which they have received. Sometimes, the trade debtors are reduced for a provision for bad debtors, i.e., those who never pay.[2] Equally, pre-payments are the mirror image of accrued charges: they represent payments in advance for future services, such as advance rental payments. Finally, cash which is only £100, in this business, is probably what is known as 'petty cash', i.e., the small (petit) quantities of ready cash which are kept in hand for day-to-day outlays. Larger transactions are usually carried out through the bank, where this business has a substantial overdraft.

HOW TRANSACTIONS AFFECT THE BALANCE SHEET

The balance sheet identity is the fundamental relationship which underlies double entry accounting and the associated financial statements which were illustrated in chapter 1. Before explaining this system in the formal, but perhaps dry and even forbidding language of algebra and double entry book-keeping, it may be helpful to develop the argument by means of a numerical illustration. This will show that the system is actually very simple, although it is often explained in technical language which makes it sound extremely complicated.

The balance sheet, it will be remembered, offers a snapshot of the firm's financial position at a single point in time, whereas the other statements introduced in chapter 1, the profit and loss account and the flow of funds statement, dealt with changes over a period of time. Thus, in order to understand the relationship between the balance sheet and the other two statements, we need to look at the consequences of transactions, and the changes which these bring about in the balance sheet.

Assume that, at time t, a business has cash of £1,000, which is capital subscribed by the proprietors. The initial balance sheet is then as follows:

Balance sheet
at t

	£		£
Proprietors' capital	1,000	Cash	1,000

The balance sheet identity holds: cash (A_t in our earlier terminology), being matched by the proprietors' claim (N_t).

At time $t+1$, the business undertakes its first trading transaction, a purchase of stock for £100 cash. Under the historic cost convention, we value stock at what was paid for it, so that there is a matching switch of assets: stock rises by £100 and cash falls by £100, leaving aggregate assets (A_{t+1}) the same, proprietors' capital (N_t) also unchanged, so that the balance sheet still balances.

Balance sheet
at $t+1$

	£		£
Proprietor's capital	1,000	Stock	100
		Cash	900
	1,000		1,000

At time $t+2$, the business makes its second trading transaction: the entire stock is sold for £150 in cash. This means that cash increases to £1,050 (i.e., £900 + £150) and the stock of £100 disappears, so that assets have now risen by £50 in aggregate. If we do nothing else, the balance sheet identity will not hold: we have accumulated £50 of assets which are not matched by claims. The logic of the balance sheet identity solves this immediately, because it says that proprietors have a residual claim, so that the £50 of surplus assets belongs to them and their claim is raised by £50. This also accords with the intuitive interpretation of the transaction: it resulted in a profit of £50, which goes to the proprietors. The balance sheet now reads as follows:

Balance sheet
at $t+2$

	£	£		£
Proprietors' capital	1,000		Cash	1,050
Add profit	50			
		1,050		
		1,050		1,050

At time $t+3$, the business replaces some of its stock by buying stock for £50 on credit, i.e., payment is not immediate. Thus stock rises by £50 on the historical cost convention (an alternative convention would lead to an immediate profit if the stock were valued higher, or a loss if it were valued lower), raising aggregate assets (A_{t+3}) by £50. This is matched by the appearance of a liability (L_{t+3}), a trade creditor, of £50 on the other side of the balance sheet, so that the identity still holds:

Balance sheet
at $t+3$

	£	£		£	£
Capital					
Proprietors' capital	1,000		*Current assets*		
Add profit	50		Stock	50	
		1,050	Cash	1,050	
Current liability					1,100
Trade creditor		50			
		1,100			1,100

The final transaction is an exchange of liabilities. At $t+4$, the firm borrows £50 on a long-term basis, to repay the creditor of £50 (this is purely an illustration: the transaction does not make much sense for a firm with £1,050 in cash, but, in practice, businesses whose current liabilities are high in relation to assets may wish to carry out a funding operation of this type). The result is that one type of liability (long-term) rises and another (current) falls, so that aggregate liabilities (L_t) remain unchanged and the balance sheet balances without further adjustment:

Balance sheet
at $t+4$

	£	£		£	£
Capital					
Proprietors' capital	1,000		*Current assets*		
Add profit	50		Stock	50	
		1,050	Cash	1,050	
					1,100
Long-term liability					
Loan		50			
		1,100			1,100

This gives us our closing balance sheet for the period. We also need to derive a profit and loss account and a flow of funds statement in order to appreciate the firm's progress over the period (as opposed to its state at the end of the period). Of these, the flow of funds statement is the most easy to assemble: we merely deduct the opening balance sheet figures from the closing balance sheet figures (although more sophisticated flows of funds statements involve more complicated detail than this):

Calculation of flows of funds
for the period t to $t+4$

	£		£
Sources		*Uses*	
Profit (50–0)	50	Stock (50–0)	50
Long-term loan (50–0)	50	Cash (1050–1000)	50
	100		100

We can arrange this information as a proper statement, in vertical format, as follows:

Flow of funds statement
from t to $t+4$

	£	£
Sources of funds		
Profit	50	
Long-term loan	50	
Total sources		100
Uses of funds		
Investment in stocks	50	
Increase in cash balance	50	
Total uses		100

Thus, the firm has become (even) more liquid: raising long-term capital and investing it in current assets.

The profit and loss account is less obviously derived from the balance sheets. For the moment, we shall adopt the cumbersome and untidy procedure of analysing each transaction which gave rise to a profit (or loss). Later, we shall learn more elegant methods of deriving profit and loss figures.

Fortunately, in our simple example, there was only one transaction which gave rise to a profit or loss. This was the second transaction (leading to the balance sheet at $t+2$), in which stock costing £100 was sold for £150, giving rise to a profit of £50. We can arrange this information as a profit and loss account as follows:

Profit and loss account
for the period t to $t+4$

	£		£
Cost of goods sold	100	Sales	150
Profit for the period	50		
	150		150

This shows a handsome profit margin ($\frac{1}{3}$) on rather low sales in relation to assets employed in the business (although we cannot assess the significance of this unless we know the length of the period of time over which the transactions took place).

A GENERALISATION

Our numerical illustration has shown clearly how the balance sheet identity ensures that each transaction involves compensating movements in balance sheet items. For example:

(1) *An increase in an asset, A,* is matched by:
    a decrease in another asset (*A*)
    or an increase in a liability (*L*)
    or an increase in proprietors' net worth (*N*)
    (A *decrease* in an asset will also be matched by changes in the other items, but with signs opposite to those listed.)

(2) *An increase in a liability, L,* is matched by:
    an increase in an asset (*A*)
    or a decrease in a liability (*L*)
    or a decrease in proprietors' net worth (*N*)
    (A *decrease* in a liability will also be matched by changes in the other items, but with opposite signs to those listed.)

A more general algebraic statement is as follows. The balance sheet identity holds at all times. Therefore:

$$A_{t+1} \equiv L_{t+1} + N_{t+1}$$
$$\text{and } A_t \equiv L_t + N_t$$

Deducting t from $t+1$, $\quad \Delta_t A \equiv \Delta_t L + \Delta_t N$

where Δ_t indicates the difference between t and $t+1$.

Each transaction is an example of the flow identity in operation. The flow of funds statement is a summation of the changes resulting from individual transactions during the period: it balances because the individual transactions each have balancing effects.

THE FULL ACCOUNTING FRAMEWORK

We have now clearly defined two accounting statements:

(1) The *balance sheet* is a statement of assets and claims at a point in time t. Algebraically:

$$A_t \equiv L_t + N_t$$

(2) The *flow of funds* statement shows how the composition of assets and claims has changed through a time period t. Algebraically:

$$\Delta_t A \equiv \Delta_t L + \Delta_t N$$

We have also referred to a third important statement, the *profit and loss account*. This fits less obviously into the framework of the balance sheet identity. However, we can track it down by thinking intuitively about the role of profit. It will be recalled that profit accrues to proprietors, i.e., it adds to N and therefore contributes to ΔN. It does not entirely explain ΔN because the proprietors may introduce new capital or withdraw capital. In order to fully explain ΔN we therefore need a fourth financial statement which includes profit but also these other items: in companies this is known as an *appropriation account* and, in unincorporated businesses, it is called the *capital account*.

We are now in a position to define these two statements more precisely:

(3) The *profit and loss account* is a statement of revenue, expenses and consequent profits (or losses) over a period of time. Algebraically:

$$P_t \equiv R_t - E_t$$

where P is profit, R is revenue and E is expenses, of the common period t.

This relationship is an identity because profit is defined as the difference between revenue and expenses. It should be noted that P, R and E are all *flows* over time, rather than stocks at a point in time.

(4) The *appropriation* or *capital account* shows how the equity interest (ordinary shareholders' stake in a company, or proprietors' net worth in an unincorporated business) has changed over a period of time. Algebraically:

$$\Delta_t N \equiv P_t + I_t - D_t$$

where $\Delta_t N$ is the change in net worth and

P is profit, as defined earlier,

I is capital introduced and

D is capital drawn out, in a common period t.

The relationship is another identity, arising from the definition of the components, and it is composed entirely of flows over the period.

The third and fourth statements, the profit and loss account and the appropriation account, do not have the simplicity or apparent comprehensiveness of the balance sheet and its dynamic counterpart, the flow of funds statement. However, the fact that they are identities is derived from the fundamental balance sheet identity, and they can be regarded as merely elaborations of that identity. The algebraically minded can demonstrate this to themselves by substituting (3) into (4) and the result into (2) to yield:

$$\Delta_t A \equiv \Delta_t L + R_t - E_t + I_t - D_t$$

The reason for deriving (4) as a separate statement is, of course, that financial statements have traditionally been prepared for proprietors (the owners of N), who have a particular interest in how their stake in the business has changed (ΔN). Moreover, proprietors and other external users (such as creditors) have a special interest in profitability, which is widely used as a measure of the past economic performance of a firm and an indication of its prospects for the future. Hence the particular attention given to the profit and loss account (3). It should be noted particularly that the importance of the profit and loss account is in its *components*, R and E (which, of course, will, in practice, be divided into relevant sub-components: different types of revenue and expense), not in the 'bottom line' measure of profit. One of the most pervasive misunderstandings of accounting is to concentrate on 'bottom line' profit and to ignore its components. This is wrong for two reasons. Firstly, accounting in general and profit measurement in particular is an imprecise art, and the profit figure usually represents a relatively small difference between two large aggregates (revenue and expense) which are subject to error. Hence, profit is very susceptible to error in its components, and an understanding of those components is essential for an informed assessment of its significance. Secondly, accounts usually relate to the past, whereas users are really interested to a large extent in the *future* prospects for profitability, which may enable their dividends, their debts, or their wages to be paid. In assessing future profitability prospects, it is important to understand the nature of the business and the recent behaviour of components of revenue and expenditure (e.g., are sales rising and are costs rising more or less in proportion?) rather than relying on naive extrapolation of a 'bottom line' net profit figure. On the other hand, the efforts of accountants in smoothing reported profits (through the way in which they operate the accrual and matching system) does make extrapolation of profit figures more reliable than it might otherwise be (there is considerable empirical evidence of this)[3], so that we should not entirely dismiss the 'bottom line', although we should be aware of its possible errors and the potentially misleading use of accounting practices through 'creative accounting'.[4]

RETROSPECT AND PROSPECT

In this chapter, we have examined the fundamental financial statement, the balance sheet, in some detail. We then showed how the balance sheet changes through time and derived the flow of funds statement as a summary of those changes over a period of time. The profit and loss account was also illustrated and defined, and the appropriation (or capital) account was defined, although not illustrated. These four financial statements form the conventional framework of financial accounting, the two most important, from an informational standpoint, being the profit and loss account and the balance sheet.

The next chapters will illustrate and explain the basic accounting *system*, from which the summary statements described in this chapter are derived. Although the financial statements are one of the primary uses of accounting information, they are the result of a great deal of work in assembling and marshalling accounting data, and their quality depends upon the quality of this underlying system. Moreover, further examination of the system may offer more insight into the properties of the final summary statements.

EXERCISES

The balance sheet

1 Derive a balance sheet from the following list of assets and claims, which includes everything other than the proprietor's capital.

Adam Ferguson
Assets and claims as at 31 October

	£
Trade debtors	600
Trade creditors	450
Cash in hand	800
Stock in trade	950
Loan from David Hume (long-term)	1,200
Motor vehicle	1,000
Bank loan (long-term)	300

2 Derive a balance sheet from the following list of assets and claims and present it in both the horizontal and the vertical formats.

William Robertson
Assets and claims as at 31 October

	£
Trade debtors	1,900
Bank overdraft	1,200
Long-term loan	600
Cash in hand	100
Stock in trade	900
Trade creditors	1,500
Freehold buildings	1,400
Proprietor's capital	1,000

Transactions and the balance sheet

3 Draw up William Robertson's balance sheet at the end of the following month, during which each of the following additional transactions occurred:

(1) He repays trade creditors £750.
(2) He sells £600 of stock for £1,200 cash.
(3) He borrows a further £400 in long-term loans.
(4) He purchases office equipment, on credit, for £300.
(5) Debtors repay £900.
(6) Robertson withdraws £200 for personal use.

All transactions involving cash were conducted through the bank.

Flow of funds

4 Draw up Robertson's summary flow of funds statement for the month of November.

Chapter 3

THE ACCOUNTING SYSTEM: ELEMENTS OF DOUBLE ENTRY ACCOUNTING

INTRODUCTION

In this chapter, we shall derive the basic double entry system which underlies the financial statements described in the previous chapter. We shall find that the double entry system is logically derived from the balance sheet identity. It is essentially a means of recording and marshalling the effect of accounting events (transactions or revaluations) in order to enable them to be summarised conveniently in the form of financial statements. Thus, conceptually, the double entry system is a logical outcome of the financial statements, although in practice the financial statements are a product of the double entry system.

The need for some system of recording and marshalling transactions may not be obvious from the examples in the previous chapters, where statements were prepared without the apparent use of such a system. This appearance was deceptive, because the examples given there had one extremely unrealistic feature: they were based on very few transactions. In practice, even very small businesses may make many transactions in a single day, and thousands within a year. It would therefore be very cumbersome for them to reconstruct their balance sheet after each transaction, as was done in the previous chapter, and even more so for a multi-national company to reconstruct its balance sheet every time it purchases a postage stamp! In this chapter, we shall illustrate a double entry system which can store information about transactions in a state from which a balance sheet can be readily derived when required. This will still leave the profit and loss account to be derived in a relatively cumbersome manner, and, in the next chapter, we shall see how the double entry system can be adapted to make profit and loss information more readily retrievable.

29

AN ILLUSTRATION

As before, we shall proceed by examining a numerical example: accounting is essentially a numerical art.

We assume that R. E. Taylor is engaged in a simple business of buying goods and selling them to the public. The opening balance sheet of the business at time *t* is as follows:

R. E. Taylor
Balance sheet
as at *t*

	£		£	£
Capital		*Current assets*		
Proprietor's capital	115	Stock	50	
Current liabilities		Trade debtors	30	
Trade creditors	25	Cash	60	
				140
	140			140

We assume that the business carries out six transactions. Example 3.1 below summarises these transactions by showing (in columnar form) the opening balance sheet (*t*) and the successive balance sheets (indicated by columns *t* + 1, etc.) following each transaction. This is a summary of the type of exercise done in chapter 2.

The transactions, and their effect, are as follows:

1 A sale of stock costing £10 for £15 in cash.
   Cash rises by £15, stock falls by £10, and the difference of £5 is profit which accrues to the proprietor. For convenience, we show the profit in a separate row from the proprietor's initial capital.
2 A purchase of stock for £20, on credit.
   Stock rises by £20 and trade creditors rise by an equal amount.
3 A debtor pays £15.
   Cash rises by £15 and trade debtors fall by an equal amount.
4 Taylor takes £25 for personal use.
   Cash falls by £25 and Taylor's capital falls by an equal amount. (Note that we do not regard this as a reduction of profit, because it is a withdrawal for private benefit rather than an expense

necessary to earn profits. If it were wages of the proprietor we *would* regard it as an expense: this shows how an element of subjective judgement enters even the apparently most simple accounting operations.)

5 Rent of £5 is paid in cash.

Cash falls by £5 and profit falls by £5, because this is assumed to be a business expense (we ignore the possibility that the rent is paid in advance, which might lead to the creation of an asset, a prepayment, rather than expense: this will be dealt with in chapter 5).

6 Sale of stock costing £30 for £50, on credit.

Stock falls by £30, trade debtors rise by £50 and the surplus of £20 is profit.

R. E. Taylor

Example 3.1. Balance sheets

Item	t	$t+1$	$t+2$	$t+3$	$t+4$	$t+5$	$t+6$
Assets							
Stock	50	40	60	60	60	60	30
Trade debtors	30	30	30	15	15	15	65
Cash	60	75	75	90	65	60	60
Total	£140	145	165	165	140	135	155
Claims							
Proprietor's capital	115	115	115	115	90	90	90
Profit (or loss)		5	5	5	5		20
Trade creditors	25	25	45	45	45	45	45
Total	£140	145	165	165	140	135	155

It will be noted that our treatment of each of these transactions obeys the balance sheet identity, profit (or loss) serving as the balancing item when changes in the other components of the balance sheet do not cancel out.

If we wish to avoid the cumbersome process of re-working the entire balance sheet after each transaction,[1] the obvious method is to record only the *changes* resulting from each transaction. These changes in balances are recorded in example 3.2. Each obeys the identity:

$$\Delta_t A \equiv \Delta_t L + \Delta_t N$$

which is, of course, the fundamental identity underlying the flow of funds statement. Thus, the net total column at the right-hand side of the example provides the ingredients of a flow of funds statement over the six transactions from t to $t+6$.

R. E. Taylor

Example 3.2. Changes in balance sheets

Item	$t+1$	$t+2$	$t+3$	$t+4$	$t+5$	$t+6$	Net total
Assets							
Stock	-10	$+20$				-30	-20
Trade debtors			-15			$+50$	$+35$
Cash	$+15$		$+15$	-25	-5		0
Total	£ $+5$	$+20$	0	-25	-5	$+20$	$+15$
Claims							
Proprietor's capital				-25			-25
Profit (or loss)	$+5$				-5	$+20$	$+20$
Trade creditors		$+20$					$+20$
Total	£ $+5$	$+20$	0	-25	-5	$+20$	$+15$

Rearranging the figures in the right-hand column, and remembering that a source of funds is an increase in a claim or a decrease in an asset (a use being the opposite), gives us the following flow of funds statement:

R. E. Taylor
Flow of funds statement
for the period t to $t+6$

	£	£
Sources of funds		
Profit for the period	20	
Increase in trade creditors	20	
Decrease in stocks	20	
Total sources		60
Uses of funds		
Withdrawn by proprietor	25	
Increase in trade debtors	35	
Total uses		60

An alternative method of arranging these records is to transpose example 3.2, to convert columns into rows. We can also add an extra row at the beginning, containing the initial balances, so that we can now add the 'change' rows to the initial balance rows in order to derive the closing balances. These operations are performed in example 3.3 which is, in fact, a primitive double entry accounting system.

It will be observed that there are two columns, a plus and a minus column, for each item. This is merely a matter of convenience, to avoid the constant use of plus and minus signs within a single column. Looking along the opening balance row, it will be seen that all of the asset balances are assigned to the plus columns and the claim balances are assigned to the minus columns. The assets are separated from the claims by the bold line in the middle of the table. This separates the assets, whose natural value is a plus, and increases in which are plus, from the claims, whose natural value is a minus, and increases in which are minus. This natural difference in sign is obtained by rearranging the balance sheet identity:

$$A_t - L_t - N_t \equiv 0$$

The rows on the table are thus defined in such a way that they sum to zero, and failure to sum to zero would indicate an error (because the balance sheet identity would not hold).

The subsequent rows in example 3.3 show, in turn, the changes in balances resulting from each transaction. Perhaps the most difficult column to understand intuitively is profit, where a minus item indicates an increase in profit, and a plus item indicates a loss. The reason for this is that profit is part of the proprietor's *claim* on the business. From the proprietor's own point of view, profit is an asset, a definite 'plus', but, from the point of view of the business, it represents an increased claim by the proprietor: the 'plus' element is the increase in net assets which gives rise to the profit.

The final two rows of example 3.3 firstly sum the plus and minus columns and secondly calculate the closing balances, which are the differences between the pairs of plus and minus columns. These closing balances are the ingredients from which we can assemble the closing balance sheet.

R. E. Taylor

Example 3.3. Double entry accounts

Transaction	Stock +	Stock −	Trade debtors +	Trade debtors −	Cash +	Cash −	Trade creditors +	Trade creditors −	Capital +	Capital −	Profit +	Profit −
Opening balance	50		30		60			25		115		
1		10			15							5
2	20							20				
3				15	15							
4						25			25			
5						5					5	
6		30	50									20
Total	70	40	80	15	90	30		45	25	115	5	25
Balance	30		65		60			45		90		20

DOUBLE ENTRY ACCOUNTING

Example 3.3 is a very rudimentary double entry accounting system. Each pair of pluses and minuses is an *account* and the whole group of accounts (example 3.3) is a *ledger*. A plus indicates what, in accounting terms, is known as a *debit* and a minus indicates a *credit*.

Thus, we can make the following definitions:

A *debit* is an increase in an asset or a decrease in a claim.
A *credit* is a decrease in an asset or an increase in a claim.

In the case of the profit and loss account, these definitions can be elaborated as follows:

A *debit* is an expense (because it reduces profit, which is a claim by the owners on the business).
A *credit* is income (because it increases profit, which is a claim).

If we have grasped these simple definitions, then we understand the basic essentials of double entry accounting. Of course, elaborate structures can be built on these simple principles, but they do not give an understanding of all the problems in accounting, any more than an understanding that stone-masonry is the art of dressing stone and fitting it together to build a structure will enable us to understand the artistic and structural complexities of a Gothic cathedral. However, stone masons who lose sight of the basic principles of their art are likely to build unsound structures, and equally it will often be instructive to reduce elaborate accounting techniques to their basic principles.

SOME FORMALITIES

In order to proceed further with double entry accounting, three useful formal techniques need to be explained. These are the trial balance, the journal entry and the T account. Each has overtones of Dickensian counting houses, where clerks would inscribe accounts in leatherbound ledgers (hence book-keeping) in long-hand, using quill pens. However, they are still useful techniques for working simple examples by hand, which is the best way of learning the fundamentals of accounting, and the principles which they embody still apply, despite the formal methods being changed by the advent of the computer.

The trial balance

If we have carried through our double entry system properly, including adding it up (or 'casting' as it used to be known, presumably because it often became a matter of fishing for the right answer), then the sum of the debit balances should always equal the sum of the credit balances. This must be true because the double entry system is based upon the fundamental balance sheet identity that assets (debits) always equal claims (credits). It is thus possible at any stage (e.g., at any row in example 3.3) to calculate the balances and confirm that they do equal credits, thus providing a check on the correct operation of the system. This will usually be done at the end of a period, before any financial statements are prepared. For example at $t + 6$ in example 3.3, we have the following trial balance:

R. E. Taylor
Trial balance
at $t + 6$

	Dr.	Cr.
Stock	30	
Trade debtors	65	
Cash	60	
Trade creditors		45
Capital		90
Profit		20
	£155	£155

It will be seen that the trial balance is merely a list of the accounts in the ledger, with the balances entered in the relevant column, Dr. indicating a debit, and Cr. indicating a credit. It will also be seen that the trial balance does indeed balance.

The journal entry

The journal entry is a very useful method of recording the debit and credit effect of a particular transaction. The journal is an old fashioned 'book of prime entry' used to initiate certain records in manual double entry book-keeping systems. Its wider use need not detain us here, although we shall return later (in chapter 8) to the concept of a book of prime entry, which is important in understanding the design and operation of accounting systems. For the moment, it is sufficient to note that a journal entry is a useful shorthand method of explaining how particular transactions are recorded: a crucial (double) question in any (double entry) accounting technique is 'what is debited, and what is credited?', and a journal entry gives us the answer to this. For example, the final transaction in the Taylor illustration (transaction 6) was sale of stock costing £30 for £50, on credit. A journal entry would summarise our treatment of this transaction as follows:[2]

	Dr.	Cr.
Trade debtor	£50	
stock		£30
profit		£20
	==	==

We follow the universal convention of 'debits on the left, credits on the right'.[3] The double horizontal lines indicate that the amounts above them sum to equal amounts in each column. There are some more elaborate formats for journal entries, in old fashioned book-keeping texts, but the simple format adopted above is adequate for the purposes of clarity, which is our sole objective here.

'T' accounts

The compact form adopted in example 3.3 can be too cramped for clear presentation of the information which is needed. Individual accounts were traditionally recorded on separate pages of a hand-written ledger, rather than being part of a single complex table, and even in the computer age it is usual (and desirable) to be able to retrieve data relating to a single account. In handwritten form, it is usual to write ledger accounts as 'T' accounts, so-called because their framework can be thought of as taking the form of a large T written on the page (the left-hand side of the T recording the debit entries and the right-hand side the credit entries).

A simple example of a T account is the following, which records R. E. Taylor's trade creditors account (details as in example 3.3):

Trade creditors

	£			£
		t	Balance b/d	25
t + 6 Balance c/d	45	*t* + 2 Stock		20
	45			45
		t + 6 Balance b/d		45

The first entry is on the credit (right-hand) side. This shows that at time *t* (usually a proper date would be given) the balance owed to creditors was £25. The expression 'b/d' means 'brought down' from the previous period: we shall see the significance of this when we consider the final entries.

The second entry, at time *t* + 2, is also a credit of £20. This was for stock purchased, and the corresponding account which was debited was 'stock': this is indicated in the narrative. In practice there might also be a cross reference to the page or number of the stock account.

The final entries are the 'closing off' of the account at the end of the period. In example 3.3, we used the crude method of summing both debit and credit columns and writing the difference between the two on the row below. In the T account format, we use the more elegant double entry method of calculating and carrying down the balance. This involves putting a balancing item 'carried down' (c/d) in order to bring the debits and credits into equality, thus 'proving' the balance. We then sum the two columns to close off the account at this point, and the balance is 'brought down' (b/d) below the summation on the opposite side to the c/d balance, i.e., the correct side for this balance (the credit side in the example given). Thus, the 'c/d' balance is really a double entry item indicating a transfer 'below the line', i.e., below the point where the account is closed off. The closing balance in the illustration is a credit balance of £45. We therefore debit the account with a £45 c/d balance, in order to enable us to close off the account at this point, and credit the account below the balancing point with a £45 b/d balance. The b/d balance is brought forward and offset against future transactions (such as cash repayments) as was the opening b/d balance of £25 at time *t*. We can now ignore all entries above this point, as the account has been closed off by double entry.

AN OVERVIEW AND A FURTHER PROBLEM

In this chapter, we have shown how we can record the effect of individual transactions or events in a compact form which enables us to assemble summary financial statements at appropriate times, without having to up-date the complete balance sheet after each transaction. This system was based on the balance sheet identity, and it therefore was a self-balancing double entry accounting system, with each asset, or change in an asset, being matched by a claim, or change in a claim. By defining assets as debits and claims as credits, our system became a form of traditional double entry book-keeping. We also explored some of the formalities of double entry book-keeping: these are matters of notation and form rather than of substance.

There was one obvious gap in the system which was illustrated (in the R. E. Taylor example): the balance sheet and flow of funds figures could readily be retrieved (the former from the opening and closing balances, the latter from the changes in those balances over the period), but the profit and loss account appeared only in summary form. We know that R. E. Taylor's accumulated profit for the period (the closing balance on the profit and loss account) was a profit (a credit balance) of £20, but it is less easy to see how that was made up. By going back over the details of the profit and loss account, we can see that transactions 1, 5 and 6 affected it, and we can rearrange the details of these transactions as:

Transaction 1:	sales £15, cost of sales £10		
" 5:		,	rent £5
" 6:	sales £50, cost of sales £30		
Total :	sales £65, cost of sales £40,		rent £5

From this, we can construct a profit and loss account (in vertical format) (see next page).

This statement is suitable for presentation to the proprietor as a statement of performance. It shows how much was sold, how much the goods (or services) cost to buy or produce, leaving a 'gross profit' or trading profit of £25. It then shows how this was reduced by overhead costs (in this example, only rent) to yield a net profit of £20.

In practice, businesses will have many more revenue and expenditure headings and many more transactions than appear in this simple example. It will therefore be extremely cumbersome and expensive to

R. E. Taylor
Profit and loss account
for the period t to $t + 6$

	£
Sales	65
Less cost of sales	40
Gross profit	25
Less rent	5
Net profit	20

'unscramble' the profit and loss data as was done above. We would prefer the double entry system to filter out such categories as sales, cost of sales and rent, producing separate totals for these rather than a single net profit figure. This is done by creating revenue and expense accounts, and the main purpose of the next chapter will be to demonstrate how this can be done in practice.

One further problem, which also affects the calculation of profit, is that we have so far concentrated only on recording transactions. We have not considered how to account for events other than transactions, notably the passage of time, which may lead to such costs as accrued expenses or depreciation. These will be considered in chapter 5.

EXERCISE

David Hume, a trader, has just started business. Listed below are his first ten transactions. You are required to record these in a double-entry system, using a simple tabular form, rather than T accounts. Prove your work by drawing up a trial balance, after recording the final transaction and Hume's closing balance sheet. Calculate what profit Hume has made during the period. State clearly any assumptions which you make.

1 Hume pays £1,000 of his own money into his business bank account to start up the business.
2 £150 is spent on stock, bought for cash.
3 £20 is paid for rent of business premises.
4 One third of the stock is sold on credit to William Robertson for £80.
5 Half of the remaining stock is sold to Adam Ferguson for £40, which is paid in cash.
6 Appleton supplies stock on credit for £120.
7 Hume pays £15 rent for his private house out of the business account.

8   William Robertson pays half of what he owes.
9   The remainder of the original stock is sold to Robertson for £70, half of which is paid in cash.
10 Adam Ferguson buys a quarter of the remaining stock for £50, on credit.

Chapter 4

THE ACCOUNTING SYSTEM: REVENUES AND EXPENSES

INTRODUCTION

The primary purpose of this chapter is, as indicated in the final section of the previous chapter, to introduce the method of preparing a detailed profit and loss account within the double entry system, by the use of revenue and expense accounts. There are, however, three subsidiary objectives. Firstly, the appropriation or capital account, which links profit, P, to change in net worth, ΔN, and which was introduced in chapter 2, will be illustrated. Secondly, the numerical illustration will relate to a manufacturer (R. T. Zan) rather than a retailer (R. E. Taylor), and this will give us the opportunity of examining how stocks and work-in-progress are recorded. Thirdly, we shall start to use the debit (dr.) and credit (cr.) notation, rather than the elementary '+' and '−' used earlier, and balances will now be carried down by the double entry 'c/d, b/d' method. We shall, however, continue to use the tabular double entry system, because its compactness has particular advantages in displaying the inter-relationships between accounts which are of particular importance in the illustrations presented here. In chapter 5, we shall resort to the T account format.

A BASIC ILLUSTRATION

Our illustration will begin by presenting accounts which have a single profit and loss account, as in chapter 3, rather than separate revenue and expense accounts.

R. T. Zan is a manufacturing business. It starts with the following list of initial assets and claims in its books:

Trial balance
at *t*

	Dr.	Cr.
Stocks		
Raw material	50	
Work-in-progress	80	
Finished goods	40	
Bank	20	
Trade debtors	30	
Trade creditors		50
Proprietor's capital		170
	£220	£220

Note that, because this is a manufacturing business, there are three types of stocks: unprocessed raw material, part-processed work-in-progress, and fully processed finished goods.

During the period, the business conducts eleven transactions, which are recorded in example 4.1 as follows:

1. A sale of goods costing £20 for £40 cash.
   Finished goods (recorded at cost) fall by £20 (a credit).
   The bank balance rises by £40 (a debit). (We assume that all cash is banked.)
   The difference of £20 is a profit (a credit to profit and loss).

2. Work-in-progress costing £30 is transferred to finished goods.
   Work-in-progress (recorded at cost) falls by £30 (a credit).
   Finished goods rise by £30 (a debit).

3. Raw material costing £20 is used for work-in-progress.
   Raw material falls by £20 (a credit).
   Work-in-progress rises by £20 (a debit).
   Note that transactions 2 and 3 are internal transfers, rather than transactions with the outside world, but the accounting system still tries to reflect the underlying physical movements (and consequent change of economic status). However, under the historical cost convention, we do not record any changes of market value which might result from these movements.

4. Raw material is bought on credit for £30.
   Raw material rises by £30 (a debit).

R. T. Zan

Example 4.1. Double entry accounts

Transaction	Raw materials		Work-in-progress		Finished goods		Bank		Trade debtors		Profit & loss		Proprietor's capital		Trade creditors	
	Dr.	Cr.	Dr.	Cr.	Dr.	Cr.	Dr.	Cr.	Dr.	Cr.	Dr.	Cr.	Dr.	Cr.	Dr.	Cr.
Opening balance b/d	50		80		40		20		30					170		50
1						20	40					20				
2				30	30											
3		20	20													
4	30															30
5								50							50	
6			20					30			10					
7			5					10			5					
8						50			50							
9							30			30						
10								20					20			
11				25	25											
Balance c/d		60		70		25	20			50	5		150		30	
Total	80	80	125	125	95	95	110	110	80	80	20	20	170	170	80	80
Closing balance b/d	60		70		25			20	50			5		150		30

Trade creditors rise by £30 (a credit).
This reflects the historical cost convention: we value the asset at what it cost, so that no profit or loss arises.

5 £50 is paid to a trade creditor.
The bank balance falls by £50 (a credit).
Trade creditors fall by £50 (a debit).

6 £30 is paid in wages, of which ⅔ is treated as a direct cost, and ⅓ as an overhead.
The bank balance falls by £30 (a credit).
Work-in-progress rises by £20 (a debit).
Profit is reduced by £10 (a debit).
The latter two entries reflect the split between work-in-progress and overheads. To the extent that we regard the wages as adding value to work-in-progress, the debit creates an asset (£20 added to work-in-progress, on the historical cost principle, in the present case). To the extent that we regard them as an overhead, the debit is an expense which reduces profit (£10 debited to the profit and loss account in this case). Obviously, the allocation between work-in-progress and expense is based on a subjective judgement and this is one inevitable source of subjectivity even within a pure historical cost system.

7 £10 is paid in rent, of which ½ is for the factory and ½ for the office.
The bank balance falls by £10 (a credit of £10).
Work-in-progress rises by £5 (a debit of £5).
Profit is reduced by £5 (a debit of £5).
The same comment applies as for transaction 6. It is assumed that factory rent adds value to work-in-progress in this industry, because processing requires time in the factory and rent buys such time: this case is more contentious than that of direct wages.

8 Goods costing £50 are sold for £50, on credit.
Finished goods are reduced by £50 (a credit).
Trade debtors rise by £50 (a debit).
In this case sales are exactly matched by cost of sales, so no profit or loss arises. Note that this transaction will not be detected if we attempt to reassemble the details of the profit and loss account by analysing only those transactions which gave rise to profits or losses, as we did in chapter 3.

9   £30 is received from a trade debtor.
       The bank balance rises by £30 (a debit).
       Trade debtors fall by £30 (a credit).

10 Zan withdraws £20 for personal use.
       The bank balance falls by £20 (a credit).
       The proprietor's capital falls by £20 (a debit).
       Note that here again there is an element of subjective judge-
       ment: if the proprietor works in the business, it might be realistic
       to classify the £20 as wages.

11 Work-in-progress costing £25 becomes finished goods.
       Work-in-progress falls by £25 (a credit).
       Finished goods rise by £25 (a debit).
       This transaction is analogous to transactions 2 and 3.

We complete the accounts in example 4.1 by the double entry
method (c/d, b/d) which was introduced at the end of the last chapter,
although later in this chapter we shall demonstrate how the example 4.1
system can be elaborated to produce more detailed information about
the components of profit and loss (example 4.3). We can prove our work
by drawing up a trial balance.

Trial balance
after transaction 11

	Dr.	Cr.
Raw materials	60	
Work-in-progress	70	
Finished goods	25	
Bank		20
Trade debtors	50	
Profit and loss		5
Proprietor's capital		150
Trade creditors		30
	£205	£205

We can arrange this information as a closing balance sheet, in
columnar form, and, by comparing it with the opening balance sheet,
derive flow of funds data, as in example 4.2:

R. T. Zan

Example 4.2 Balance sheet and flow of funds data

Account	Balance sheets		Flow of funds
Assets	Opening (*t*)	closing (*t*+11)	((*t*+11)−*t*)
Raw materials	50	60	+10
Work-in-progress	80	70	−10
Finished goods	40	25	−15
Trade debtors	30	50	+20
Bank	20	−20	−40
Total	£ 220	£ 185	£ −35
Claims			
Trade creditors	50	30	−20
Proprietor's capital	170	155	−15
Total	£ 220	£ 185	£ −35

We can present the balance sheet as follows:

R. T. Zan
Balance sheet
as at *t*+11

	£	£
Current assets		
Stocks and work-in-progress	155	
Trade debtors	50	
		205
less current liabilities		
Trade creditors	30	
Bank overdraft	20	
		50
Net current assets		155
Financed by:		
Proprietor's capital: opening balance	170	
Add profit for the period	5	
	175	
Less Drawings	20	
Closing balance		155

The associated flow of funds statement would be:

R. T. Zan
Flow of funds statement
for the period _t_ to _t_+11

Sources of funds	£	£
Reduction in stocks (*note* 1)	15	
Bank (*note* 2)	40	
Profit of the period	15	
Total		60

Uses of funds		
Increase in trade debtors	20	
Increase in trade creditors	20	
Proprietor's drawings	20	
Total		60

Note 1   Raw materials increased by £10.
Work-in-progress fell by £10 and finished goods fell by £15.

Note 2   Cash in bank of £20 was spent, and an additional £20 was borrowed on overdraft.

The next problem which arises is that of preparing the profit and loss account, and we might add also the preparation of the proprietor's capital account: our analysis of the change in the balance on this account into profit of the period and proprietor's drawings was based on informal observation and would not have been so easy had there been many transactions on this account (e.g., including new capital introduced also).

We can first proceed to assemble the profit and loss information by the informal method used at the end of chapter 3. We note that transactions 1, 6 and 7 led to changes in profit, and additionally note that transaction 8 led to the creation of revenue and expense, although the two offset one another. We analyse these transactions as follows:

Transaction	Sales	Cost of goods sold	Overhead expenses Rent	Wages
1	40	20		
6				10
7			5	
8	50	50		
Total	£90	£70	£5	£10

From this information, we can construct a profit and loss account:

R. T. Zan
Profit and loss account
for the period t to t+11

	£	£
Sales	90	
Less cost of goods sold	70	
Gross profit		20
Less overhead expenses:		
Rent	5	
Wages	15	
		15
Net profit		5

This produces a 'bottom line' figure of net profit (or P in our earlier notation). In order to reconcile profit to change in net worth (ΔN) on the balance sheet, we need an appropriation or proprietor's capital account. In this case, we have already provided a capital account as part of the balance sheet. This too was based on informal adjustment (the net change in proprietor's capital between the two balance sheets was a fall of £15, but we need to look elsewhere to find that this was composed of profit of £5, less drawings of £20), and it would be convenient if this information, in addition to profit and loss information, emerged naturally from the double entry system.

REVENUE AND EXPENSE ACCOUNTS

In order to adapt the double entry system to give us full details of the individual revenue and expense items which make up the profit and loss account, we place the analysis which we have just done within the double entry framework. We thus need a sales account, which will have credit entries (summing to £90 in our example), because sales increase profit (and therefore, ultimately, the proprietor's claim). We also need a cost of sales account (summing to £70 in our example), and overhead expense accounts for rent (£5) and wages (£10), all of which will be debits, because they reduce profit (and therefore, ultimately, the proprietor's claim).

In order to incorporate these new accounts into the double entry system, we no longer enter the effect of transactions direct to the profit and loss account. The new treatments are probably best illustrated by example. Transaction 1, it will be recalled, was a sale of goods costing £20 for £40 in cash. Our original double entry was, in journal form:

	Dr.	Cr.
Bank	£40	
Stock		£20
Profit and loss		£20
	==	==

Our new double entry is:

	Dr.	Cr.
Bank	£40	
Sales		£40
Cost of sales	£20	
Stock		£20
	==	==

Thus, instead of creating a single credit (profit) to profit and loss, of £20, we have created a separate debit (cost of sales), of £20, as a counterpart of the loss of stock, and a credit (sales), of £40, as a counterpart to the receipt of the cash: the net effect is, in double entry terms, the same (a net credit of £20).

Transactions 6 and 7 are also treated differently under the new method: the expense debits (for wages £10 and rent £5 respectively) are now debited to separate accounts rather than direct to profit and loss:

	Dr.	Cr.
Work-in-progress	£20	
Profit and loss	£10	
Bank		£30
	==	==

It is now:

	Dr.	Cr.
Work-in-progress	£20	
Wages	£10	
Bank	=	£30

and rent (transaction 7) is treated in a similar manner.

Transaction 8 is similar to transaction 1, and its treatment is changed similarly. It was formerly:

	Dr.	Cr.
Trade debtors	£50	
Stock of finished goods	=	£50

It is now:

	Dr.	Cr.
Trade debtors	£50	
Sales		£50
Cost of goods sold	£50	
Stock of finished goods	=	£50

These transactions are entered in the new format in the upper part of example 4.3 (above the single horizontal line) which replaces the direct profit and loss account entries in example 4.1. We also introduce a drawings account, to which the £20 capital withdrawal by the proprietor is debited rather than being debited direct to the proprietor's capital account. This clears the way for the capital account to become a comprehensive summary statement of changes in the proprietor's interest (ΔN in our formal notation). The need for such a summary is made less obvious in our simple illustration with only one capital withdrawal and four transactions affecting profit and loss, than it would be in a more realistic example, but the reader should be grateful for being spared the tedious details of a more realistic example.

The above eight accounts replace the existing profit and loss account and proprietor's account, recorded in example 4.1.

Having entered the transactions in their new format in example 4.3, we have accumulated debits on three expense accounts, wages, rent and

Example 4.3

Transaction	Manufac-turing and trading account		Profit & loss		Proprietor's capital account		Overhead wages		Office rent		Sales		Cost of goods sold		Drawings	
	Dr.	Cr.	Dr.	Cr.	Dr.	Cr.	Dr.	Cr.	Dr.	Cr.	Dr.	Cr.	Dr.	Cr.	Dr.	Cr.
Opening balance						170										
1																
6							10					40	20			
7									5							
8												50	50		20	
10																
T/R trading account	70	90		20		170					90	90	70	70		
T/R P/L	20		10				10	10								
T/R P/L			5						5	5						
T/R appropriation A/C			5		20	5										
Balance c/d					155										20	
					£175	£175										£20
Balance b/d						155										

cost of goods sold (£10, £5 and £70 respectively: totals are summed in the first row below the single horizontal line, for convenience), and a credit on one expense account, sales (£90). In addition, we have a debit on the drawings account (£20), which will ultimately need to be charged against the capital account.

The way in which we deal with these new balances is to *transfer* them to the relevant account. The revenue and expense accounts are really parts of the profit and loss account, serving the role of convenient accumulation accounts, the totals of which are finally transferred to the main account (which, so far, has no entries). The drawings account serves a similar role in relation to the capital account, as would a capital introduced account, if the proprietor paid capital into the business on a regular basis.

The mechanics of transfers are simple double entry. If we wish to transfer a debit balance of £x from account a to account b, we simply credit account a with £x and debit account b with £x. A transfer entry is prefaced by the abbreviation T/R. Two examples occur in example 4.3, in the row marked T/R trading account. These represent transfers of sales and cost of goods sold, respectively, to a new account, entitled manufacturing and trading account,[1] where gross profit is calculated. We transfer sales by debiting the sales account and crediting the manufacturing and trading account with £90, the total sales for the period, thus leaving no balance in the sales account, which is closed off for the period (as indicated by the double horizonal lines). We transfer cost of goods sold by crediting that account and debiting the manufacturing and trading account with the total cost of £70, thus enabling the cost of goods sold account to be closed off for the period.

We now have a manufacturing and trading account which has a credit of £90, for sales, and a debit of £70, for cost of sales. The difference, a net credit balance of £20, is gross profit for the period. We now transfer this to the profit and loss account, by debiting manufacturing and trading account with £20 (thus enabling this account to be closed off), and crediting £20 to the profit and loss account. We also transfer the two overhead expense accounts to profit and loss. Firstly, overhead wages are credited and profit and loss debited with £10, and, secondly, office rent is credited and profit and loss is debited with £5. These transfers enable us to close off the two expense accounts.

We now have a net credit balance of £5 on the profit and loss account, which represents the net profit of the period. The final operations are to transfer the net profit and the drawings balance to the proprietor's capital account. Firstly, the net profit is transferred by debiting the profit and loss account with £5, to close off the account, and crediting the proprietor's capital account. Secondly, the drawings account balance is transferred by crediting drawings with £20, to close off the account, and debiting the proprietor's capital account with £20. The proprietor's capital account now has a net credit balance of £155, and this balance is carried down by the double entry method, to show the net effect of all these transactions on the proprietor's interest in the business.

DERIVATION AND PRESENTATION OF THE PROFIT AND LOSS ACCOUNT

The system presented in example 4.3 is not only elegant but is also extremely efficient in marshalling large numbers of transactions. We can derive a profit and loss account in horizontal format simply by copying out the manufacturing and trading account and the profit and loss account from example 4.3, together with the narrative descriptions which would attach to each item ('sales', etc.) in a proper T account format:

R. T. Zan
Profit and loss account
for the period t to $t+11$

	£		£
Cost of goods sold	70	Sales	90
Gross profit, carried down	20		
	90		90
Overhead wages	10	Gross profit, brought down	20
Office rent	5		
	15		
Net profit	5		
	20		20

In this case, we have included the manufacturing and trading account as the upper part of the profit and loss account, which is quite common practice, although the two could be treated as separate statements, each with its own heading.

The proprietor's capital account can also be derived, in horizontal format, by copying out the ledger account and adding an appropriate narrative description:

R. T. Zan
Proprietor's capital account
for the period t to $t+11$

	£		£
Drawings for the period	20	Opening balance (at t), brought forward	170
Closing balance (at $t+11$) carried forward	155	Profit for the period	5
	175		175

This contains the information which we earlier obtained on an informal basis and incorporated in the balance sheet at $t + 11$. In a company, only the final balance (or balances where there are various categories of shares and reserves) would appear in the balance sheet, and the details of changes would appear in the appropriation account, which is typically merged in with the profit and loss account.[2]

We can rearrange these statements in vertical format, as follows:

R. T. Zan
Profit and loss account
for the period t to $t+11$

	£	£
Sales	90	
Less cost of goods sold	70	
Gross profit		20
Less expenses:		
Wages	10	
Rent	5	
		15
Net profit for the period		5

R. T. Zan
Proprietor's capital account
for the period *t* to *t*+11

	£
Balance at *t*, brought forward	170
Add net profit for the period	5
	175
Less drawings for the period	20
Balance at *t* + 11, carried forward	155

REVIEW

In this chapter, we have seen how the rudimentary double entry system introduced in chapter 3, which recorded changes in balance sheet items, can be extended to record separately the details of the profit and loss account and other components of change in proprietor's interest (ΔN). The profit and loss detail was obtained by accumulating various items of revenue and expense in separate accounts, the totals of which were transferred to the profit and loss account at the end of the period. The details of the other sources of change in proprietor's interest, such as capital introduced (a direct increase in N) and capital withdrawn (a direct decrease in N, described as 'drawings' in our illustration), can also be accumulated in separate accounts for transfer in total to the capital account (or appropriation account in the case of a company) at the end of the period.

As a result of the creation of revenue and expense accounts, we have a more complicated definition of debit and credit:

A *debit* is an increase in an asset, a decrease in a claim *or* an expense.
A *credit* is a decrease in an asset, an increase in a claim *or* revenue.

Strictly, these are not new definitions of debit and credit, but elaborations of the old ones: an expense decreases profit, decreasing proprietor's net worth (N), which is a claim, and revenue increases profit, thus increasing the proprietor's claim. It is important to bear this in mind when faced with the apparent intuitive conflict between a debit being an increase in an asset or a reduction in a liability (which sound good things), or an expense (which sounds a bad thing). From the point of view of the *firm*, the expense relieves the firm of part of its residual obligation to the proprietor, so that it reduces a claim in the same way as does a reduction in a liability. The double entry system is neutral as to whether particular changes in balances are good or bad things, and is instead merely concerned with maintaining the balance sheet identity. From the *proprietor's* point of view, it is, of course, important that his own stake (N), which is an asset (or debit) in his personal accounts,[3] should be as high as possible. It is for this reason that we have paid such careful attention to assembling the detail necessary to explain how the proprietor's claim has changed during the period, and, in particular, how the profit and loss on the firm's activities has contributed to this.

We have now examined the main accounting statements and the double entry system from which they are derived. The one remaining gap in the discussion is the application of the matching system: how expenses are accrued at the end of a period so that the charge relates to the revenue earned, and how the cost of fixed assets is allocated as an expense over their life-time, by the method of depreciation. This is the main topic of chapter 5.

EXERCISE

Grantchester Gaskets is a small manufacturing firm. From the following information (see overleaf) prepare double entry records for the month, and summary accounts, including a profit and loss account and a balance sheet.

Assets and liabilities, 1 January 19__

	£
Stock (at cost)	
Raw materials	350
Work-in-progress	250
Finished goods	300
Trade debtors	500
Trade creditors	320
Cash at bank	390
Equipment (at cost)	800
Proprietor's capital	2,270

Transactions

January	3	Sold goods costing £80 on credit	100
	6	Bought raw materials on credit	90
	7	Paid wages	40
	11	Received payment from debtors	200
	14	Paid wages	40
	16	Work-in progress completed and transferred to finished goods, cost	120
	21	Paid wages	40
	23	Paid creditors	120
	24	Sold on credit, stock costing £200 for	280
	28	Paid wages	40
	31	Paid monthly rent (in arrears)	20

During the month raw materials costing £20 were used for manufacturing purposes.

Half the wages and half the rent are assumed to add to the value of work-in-progress. The remainder is written off as an expense.

Required

(a) Prepare the double entry accounts in 'T' form.

(b) Open separate expense and revenue accounts for the components of the profit and loss account.

(c) No depreciation of equipment is to be allowed for.

Chapter 5

THE ACCOUNTING SYSTEM: ACCRUALS, PREPAYMENTS AND DEPRECIATION

INTRODUCTION

We have now devised a double entry accounting system capable of accumulating details about *transactions* in a form suitable for assembling the summary financial statements. We have so far avoided the problem of *matching*, i.e., of charging only those costs in a period which were incurred in earning the revenues of that period. This problem has two practical manifestations: firstly, the allocation of short-term expenses between pairs of adjacent periods, and, secondly, the allocation of the cost of long-term (fixed) assets over the periods spanned by their useful lives. Both are aspects of the same central problem, of matching, but the different time scales involved lead to different techniques: accruals and prepayments in the case of short-term expenses, and depreciation in the case of fixed assets. We deal with the short-term problem first.

ACCRUAL AND PREPAYMENT OF SHORT-TERM EXPENSES

It will often be the case that, at the end of a period, some expenses will have been paid which bring benefit in a subsequent period. Equally, some of the benefits derived in the current period may have been paid for in a previous period. This is a situation involving the *prepayment* of an expense, and it is dealt with by treating the prepayment as an asset at the end of the period in which the payment is made, and then converting the asset to an expense (both are debits, so this is merely a matter of classification) in the following period, in which the benefit is received.

As an example, let us assume that a firm paid an insurance premium of £1,000 in the previous accounting year, half of which related to the

59

current year. Half way through the current year, £1,200 is paid as the premium for the next twelve months, only half of which has expired at the end of the accounting year.

The simplest way to record this is as follows:

Insurance

		£			£
1 January	Balance b/d	500	31 December	Profit and loss	1,100
30 June	Bank	1,200	31 December	Balance c/d	600
		1,700			1,700
1 January	Balance b/d	600			

The insurance account is an expense account, so that the expense for the year is transferred to profit and loss. However, we also use it, in this case, as an asset account, to the extent that the benefit of the expenditure has not yet been received. Thus, at the beginning of the year, we have an opening balance (b/d) of £500, which is the prepaid amount brought forward from the previous year: this will appear as an asset (a prepayment of £500) in the opening balance sheet. During the year, the payment of £1,200 is debited to the insurance account, the corresponding credit being to the bank. At the end of the year we calculate the proportion of the payment which is for future benefit: half of £1,200, giving £600. This is treated as an asset and is therefore carried down as a balance at the year end (as was the £500 at the beginning of the year). The residue (£1,100) is treated as an expense and is therefore transferred to the profit and loss account. Thus, although the £600 prepayment is described as a balance, the residual item which enables us to close off the account is really the £1,100 charge to profit and loss. This can be explained as follows:

	£
Prepayment from previous year	500
Add payment during the year	1,200
	1,700
Less prepayment for the next year	600
Cost charged for the year	1,100

An alternative method of implementing the same process is to transfer the prepayment balance to another account (where it might be accumulated with other prepayments) to maintain a separation between asset and expense accounts. If we do this, we must remember to 'write off' the prepayment when it is used, by transferring it back to the expense account, which now reads:

Insurance

		£			£
1 January	T/R prepayment	500	31 December	T/R prepayment	600
30 June	Bank	1,200	31 December	Profit and loss	1,100
		1,700			1,700

and the associated prepayments account reads:

Prepayments

		£			£
1 January	Balance b/d	500	1 January	T/R insurance	500
31 December	T/R insurance	600	31 December	Balance c/d	600
		1,100			1,100
1 January	b/d	600			

The insurance account merely has transfers (T/R) to and from prepayments rather than balances carried down (c/d) and brought down (b/d). The prepayments account serves as the recipient of these transfers and as a vehicle for carrying down the balances, which are then transferred back to the expense account.

The mirror image of the prepayment is the accrued expense. This arises when an expense has been incurred but has not been recorded by the system, e.g., typically because an invoice (e.g., a telephone bill) has not been received, and sometimes because expenses are recorded when they are paid for rather than (as in the case of trade creditors) by recording transactions when the goods (or services) change hands and the liability to pay is incurred.

The treatment of accrued creditors is the same as for prepayments with the signs (debit or credit) reversed. We can illustrate this as follows. Assume that a firm had accumulated £100 electricity charges at the beginning of January. During the year, it pays quarterly bills of

£300, £400, £250 and £350. The final bill relates to the quarter ended 1 December. The bill rendered for the following quarter (ended 1 March) was for £390. It is considered appropriate to apportion this equally between months, so that £130 related to December. The electricity account for the accounting year ended 31 December[1] can be as follows:

Electricity

		£			£
February	Bank	300	1 January	Balance b/d	100
May	Bank	400	31 December	Profit and loss	1,330
August	Bank	250			
December	Bank	350			
31 December	Balance c/d	130			
		1,430			1,430
			1 January	Balance b/d	130

The initial credit balance (£100) represents the amount accumulated at the beginning of the year, the bank payments are the amounts paid during the year to clear the initial balance and to pay for subsequent supplies, and the closing balance (£130) represents the amount used but not paid for at the end of the year. The charge to profit and loss is made up as follows:

	£
Paid during the year (bank)	1,300
Less owed at the beginning of the year	100
Used and paid for during the year	1,200
Add used but not paid for at the end of the year	130
Cost of electricity used during the year	1,330

This treatment is exactly analogous with the first treatment illustrated for insurance, but the present case involves accrued liabilities (credit balances) rather than prepayments (debit balances).

We can also implement an alternative method of dealing with accrued expenses which is analogous with the alternative treatment of prepayments:

Electricity

		£			£
February	Bank	300	1 January	T/R accrued expenses	100
May	Bank	400	31 December	Profit and loss	1,330
August	Bank	250			
December	Bank	350			
31 December	T/R accrued expenses	130			
		1,430			1,430

Accrued expenses

		£			£
1 January	T/R electricity	100	1 January	Balance b/d	100
31 December	Balance c/d	130	31 December	T/R electricity	130
		230			230
			1 January	Balance b/d	130

The electricity account is now a pure expense account, the accrual adjustments being transferred to the accrued expenses account, where the balances are carried down, for subsequent transfer back to the expense account in the following period.

Before we leave the problems of accruing short-term expenses, it is important to note that we have, somewhat glibly, assumed that the apportionment of expenses is a fairly simple matter and can be done with reasonable accuracy on the basis of assuming that expenses accrue at a roughly constant rate through time. Because of the short-term nature of these expenses, such an assumption may be acceptable and may not lead to material errors in many cases. However, it is important to note three things. Firstly, it is not necessarily the case that certain items accrue at a steady rate through time, e.g., electricity costs will be reduced by holiday closures and increased by cold weather and short days. Secondly, even if the cost accrues at a steady rate, the benefit does not necessarily do so, and it is the benefit (revenue generated) to which cost should be matched (e.g., we may pay rent for property for a fixed period but use it to different extents at different times). Thirdly, even if the benefit accrues at a constant rate, economic theory tells us that a future benefit is worth less than an immediate benefit (because £1 now can be invested at the rate of interest to earn a greater future sum).

Thus, even in the case of constant benefit, there is a case for allocating a greater proportion of the cost to the earlier part of the period. However, these problems are likely to be less important in the case of short-term accruals because of the short periods over which the accruals take place. The problem of allocation to time periods is more serious in relation to the depreciation of fixed assets, which will typically involve allocation over a span of several periods.

DEPRECIATION

In the case of short-term expenses, the initial assumption was that any expenditure was an expense of the period. The insurance and electricity payments were debited initially to expense accounts, where they were *prima facie* assumed to be expenses of the period, subject to adjustments for accrued expenses or prepayments, which were made by creating closing balances.

By contrast, in the case of fixed assets, the *prima facie* assumption is that expenditure gives rise to an asset, rather than an expense. An adjustment is made at the end of the period by 'writing down' the asset (creating a credit balance) and charging the profit and loss account (a debit) with depreciation. The amount of depreciation should represent an allocation of the total cost to that period, based on the matching principle.

As a simple illustration, let us assume that a firm pays £20,000 for a fixed asset on 1 January. It is decided by 31 December, when the annual accounts are prepared, that 20 per cent of the original cost should be charged as depreciation. The following is the simplest, but not necessarily the best, way of recording this:

Fixed asset

	£		£
1 January Bank	20,000	31 December Profit and loss	4,000
		31 December Balance c/d	16,000
	20,000		20,000
1 January Balance b/d	16,000		

In this illustration, the depreciation charge is debited direct to the profit and loss account. We might prefer to do this in two stages: firstly debiting a depreciation expense account, where depreciation charges on other assets can also be accumulated, and secondly transferring the aggregate depreciation charge on all assets (or all assets of a similar type) to the profit and loss account.

Another feature of the illustration is that the balance carried down (£16,000) represents net carrying amount, i.e., cost (£20,000) less accumulated depreciation to date (£4,000). We might prefer to keep these items separate, because original cost is a much 'harder' (more objective) piece of information than depreciation, which is very much an estimate. We could deal with this problem by carrying down cost and depreciation balances on opposite sides of the same fixed asset account. This would result in the following:

Fixed asset

		£			£
1 January	Bank	20,000	31 December	Depreciation charge	4,000
31 December	Balance (depreciation) c/d		31 December	Balance (cost) c/d	20,000
		4,000			
		24,000			24,000
1 January	Balance (cost) b/d	20,000	1 January	Balance (depreciation) b/d	4,000

Thus, we can now easily retrieve the type of information given in the balance sheet in chapter 2.

Fixed asset	£
Cost	20,000
Less depreciation	4,000
	16,000

The depreciation charge of £4,000 is now debited to a separate expense account which will be transferred, in total, to profit and loss. The depreciation balance is not an expense but a provision for diminution in the value of the fixed asset, i.e., it is a sort of negative asset, which is deducted from the cost of the fixed asset in order to derive its carrying amount. In the first year (illustrated here) it equals the charge for the year. In subsequent years, it will grow as further annual provisions are added.

A more usual method of carrying the cost of fixed assets and the depreciation provision is to show them in separate accounts:

Fixed asset, at cost

		£			£
1 January	Bank	20,000	31 December	Balance c/d	20,000
		20,000			20,000
1 January	Balance b/d	20,000			

Depreciation provision

		£			£
31 December	Balance c/d	4,000	31 December	Depreciation charge	4,000
		4,000			4,000
			1 January	Balance b/d	4,000

The depreciation provision is a credit balance carried forward to be added to in future years. The depreciation charge account, on the other hand, has a debit balance which is written off this year by being transferred to profit and loss:

Depreciation charge

	£			£
31 December Depreciation provision	4,000	31 December Profit and loss		4,000
	4,000			4,000

This example completes the discussion of the formal record-keeping aspects of depreciation and the treatment of fixed assets within the double entry system. However, this merely explains how we shuffle the numbers once we have decided on the amount of depreciation, and the method for deciding on the amount is crucial to the usefulness of the depreciation figure as information.

In practice, accountants have a number of rules of thumb for deciding on the allocation of depreciation over an asset's useful life. The most popular are the straight line method and the reducing balance method.

The *straight line* method allocates an *equal amount* of depreciation over each year of the asset's life. Hence, the net carrying amount of the asset decreases linearly through time, i.e., if successive written down values are plotted on a graph, they will be on a straight line. Equally, accumulated depreciation increases linearly (which is the cause of the linear decrease in written down value). The formula for straight line depreciation is:

$$D = \frac{C - S}{L}$$

where D is the amount of original cost written off in each period
      C is the cost of the asset
      S is scrap value
      L is life time, expressed in number of periods.

The initial depreciation in our example is £4,000 p.a., with cost at £20,000. If we assume that depreciation is assessed on a straight line basis, the annual charge will continue to be £4,000 until the asset is scrapped. For example, if the assumed life were three years, this would imply an annual charge of £4,000 for three years, followed by scrapping (or second-hand sale) for £8,000.[2]

The *reducing balance* method attempts to allow for cases in which the greater part of the benefit of the asset is received early in its life. It thus charges a *constant proportion of the written down value* of the asset as depreciation in each year of its life. Thus, in our example, if the depreciation rate were 20 per cent on a reducing balance basis, we would write off £4,000 in the first year (0.2 × £20,000), but only £3,200 in the second year (0.2 × (£20,000 − £4,000)), £2,560 in the third year (0.2 × (£20,000 − £4,000 − £3,200)) and so on until the asset's useful life ends, by which time it should be written down to its anticipated scrap value. In order to calculate the appropriate proportionate rate at which depreciation should be charged on a reducing balance rate, in order to reduce cost to anticipated scrap value over the estimated life, we use the algebraic relationship:[3]

$$d = 1 - \sqrt[L]{\frac{S}{C}}$$

where d is proportionate depreciation rate, and L, S and C are defined as before.

Two features of this relationship should be noted. Firstly, the nature of proportionate decline in the residual balance is that it approaches zero asymptotically, i.e., it eventually moves infinitesimally close, but never quite reaches it. Hence, the formula cannot deal with zero (or negative) scrap values. This problem is often dealt with by substituting a small nominal scrap value (say £1) for zero, although this is not an entirely satisfactory solution, given the sensitivity of the depreciation rate to the arbitrarily chosen scrap value. Secondly, we should note that, for any given proportionate rate of depreciation, the straight line method will give the more rapid write off, implying a shorter life or a higher scrap value, or both. Thus, for similar assets, we would expect the proportionate rate to be higher under the reducing balance method than under the straight line method.

There is a variety of other methods of allocating depreciation costs between periods, which appear in more advanced texts on accounting methods. All of them are essentially arbitrary, because depreciation is a method of allocating a single outlay (the cost of the fixed asset) over a number of periods, so that depreciation is a joint cost of several periods.[4] A possible resolution of this problem is to revalue the asset at the end of every period, so that depreciation represents the difference between opening and closing values, i.e., the loss (or gain, when asset values appreciate) from holding the asset in the firm during the period. However, this takes us out of the realm of traditional cost-based accounting and into the potentially fruitful but not yet practical world of current value accounting. The same is true of the associated (but not identical) idea of 'economic depreciation', which bases the valuation of an asset (and the associated periodic change in value, giving rise to depreciation or appreciation of the asset) on the present value of the future benefits to be derived from holding the asset: this idea lay behind our earlier suggestion that, in accruing prepayments, we might have regard to the fact that, when the rate of interest is positive, a future benefit is worth less than an immediate benefit.

We can learn two things from this discussion. Firstly, the assessment of depreciation within the conventional accounting framework is both arbitrary (depending on the rule of thumb adopted, such as straight line) and subjective (depending on estimates of future useful life and scrap value). This is important because depreciation can be an important charge in the profit and loss account and depreciated assets can be a significant element in the balance sheet. Secondly, even a brief discussion of depreciation brings into question the appropriateness of the historical cost assumption. We shall return briefly to the subject of alternative valuation methods in chapter 7.[5]

For the moment, we must leave these broader theoretical issues and return to a concrete example which will enable us to consolidate our understanding of how prepayments, accrued expenses and depreciation are recorded in the double entry system.

The objectives of this illustration are threefold. Firstly, to revise the double entry system which we have already learned, including the creation of separate revenue and expense accounts; secondly, to illustrate a set of ledger accounts in T account form; thirdly, to illustrate the method of dealing with accruals, prepayments and depreciation.

Dr Seatham Rythe[6] is a dentist. He set up business on 1 January, subsequently making several transactions. The effect of these, in journal form, is as follows:

Transaction (1): £1,500 was spent on new equipment, using a bank overdraft:

	Dr.	Cr.
Equipment	£1,500	
Bank		£1,500

An asset has been created and is balanced by an equal liability. Subsequent transactions will all be recorded in journal form and then, later, this will be translated into T accounts.

Transaction (2): A year's rent was paid in advance, on 1 January, using his private bank account:

	Dr.	Cr.
Rent	£300	
Capital introduced		£300

Rent is an expense account, ultimately to be transferred to profit and loss, and capital introduced is a subsidiary account of the proprietor's capital account, to which it will ultimately be transferred.

Transaction (3): he pays £50 from his private bank account for a stock of materials. The effect is:

	Dr.	Cr.
Cost of materials	£50	
Capital introduced		£50

Again, we debit an expense account and credit capital introduced. Note that we regard materials immediately as an expense, not as an asset (as in the R. T. Zan case). This is because we are dealing with a service business, where materials are a small component of cost, and stocks are likely to be small. It is therefore not worth maintaining 'continuous inventory' records as in the R. T. Zan case, in which purchases enter stock and are charged as expenses against profit only when they are used. Instead, we regard purchases as an expense and make an adjustment for closing stocks at the end of the period, which are treated as a prepayment for future benefit (transaction (11)).

The above transactions initiate the business on 1 January. During the subsequent year, the following six transactions ((4) to (9)) take place:

Transaction (4): The receptionist is paid £600 for the year. We assume that all receipts and payments pass through the bank account.

	Dr.	Cr.
Wages	£600	
Bank		£600

Wages, an expense account, is debited, and the bank account is credited (i.e., money drawn out).

Transaction (5): Paid an insurance premium of £30 on 1 January.

	Dr.	Cr.
Insurance	£30	
Bank		£30

Again, an expense is debited and the bank credited. The expense account will be adjusted later to allow for a prepayment.

Transaction (6): Further materials were purchased for £700, of which £500 was paid from the business bank account, the remainder being still owing at the end of the year.

	Dr.	Cr.
Cost of materials	£700	
Trade creditors		£700
Trade creditors	£500	
Bank		£500

There are two stages in this transaction (or, more strictly, series of transactions). Firstly, the goods are bought on credit, so that the expense account, cost of materials, is debited (in conformity with the treatment of transaction (3)) and the liability (trade creditors) is credited. Secondly, the liability is paid (in part), so that trade creditors are debited and the bank credited, i.e., a liability has fallen and an asset has fallen (or, if the bank account is overdrawn at the time, a liability has risen).

Transaction (7): Fees charged to patients during the year were £4,000, of which £3,500 was received during the year:

	Dr.	Cr.
Debtors	£4,000	
Fees earned		£4,000
Bank	£3,500	
Debtors		£3,500

As with transaction (6), this transaction (or series of transactions) has two distinct stages: a credit transaction, followed by partial cash settlement.

Transaction (8): Electricity charges amounting to £95 were paid during the year:

	Dr.	Cr.
Electricity	£95	
Bank		£95

This is an expense transaction like (5) above, although in this case we shall make a late adjustment for an accrued liability rather than a prepayment.

Transaction (9): During the year, Rythe drew £1,950 out of the business for personal use:

	Dr.	Cr.
Drawings	£1,950	
Bank		£1,950

The drawings account is the mirror-image of the capital introduced account (transactions (2) and (3)). It too will ultimately be transferred to the proprietor's capital account, but as a debit (reduction in proprietor's claim) rather than as a credit.

This completes the list of transactions completed during the year. We now turn to four items of information about the state of the business at the end of the year which will require adjustment before the financial statements are prepared.

(10): The insurance premium (transaction (5)) covered eighteen months from the date of payment. It is therefore thought appropriate to treat one third of the premium (£10) as a prepayment.

	Dr.	Cr.
Prepayments	£10	
Insurance		£10

We could, alternatively, use the c/d, b/d balance method. The method illustrated is clearer if, as here, we wish to make the adjustment before (rather than simultaneously with) the transfer of the expense to profit and loss.

(11): The accumulated liability for electricity at the end of the year was £25.

	Dr.	Cr.
Electricity	£25	
Accrued liabilities		£25

Again, we have chosen to open a separate account for the balance, as in (10).

(12): At the end of the year, 10 per cent depreciation is to be written off the equipment.

	Dr.	Cr.
Depreciation charge	£150	
Accumulated depreciation		£150

We have debited an expense account and credited the provision, which will be carried forward as a credit balance (to be offset against the debit balance, cost of equipment, in the balance sheet) and accumulated with subsequent provisions.

(13): The stock of materials at the end of the year is £80.

	Dr.	Cr.
Stock	£80	
Cost of materials		£80

We have debited stock, thus recording an asset, and credited cost of materials, thus recording a reduction in the expense balance, which will be transferred from this account to profit and loss. Stock is thus a form of prepayment and its treatment here is directly analogous with the treatment of the insurance prepayments in (10) above. If we had used the 'continuous inventory' method of recording stock, as in the Zan example of the previous chapter, the appropriate analogy would have been with depreciation ((12) above): the stock purchase would have been regarded initially as giving rise to an asset rather than an expense and would have been written off (by transfer to work-in-progress, finished goods and ultimately cost of sales) as it was used up.

We now enter these transactions in a ledger, in T account form. When the entries are complete, we check that they are correct by drawing up a trial balance (this also might be done after transaction (9) and before the closing adjustments). We then transfer the revenue and expense balances to the profit and loss account and the profit and loss balance, together with drawings and capital introduced to the proprietor's capital account. This gives us all the information necessary to prepare the financial statements. Below, we show the T accounts, after all these operations, followed by two trial balances, one drawn up before the transfers and the final one drawn up after the transfers. Transfers are, as in the previous chapter, prefaced by the abbreviation T/R.

Dr Seatham Rythe: Ledger

Bank

		£			£
(7)	Debtors	3,500	(1)	Equipment	1,500
			(4)	Wages	600
			(5)	Insurance	30
			(6)	Trade creditors	500
			(8)	Electricity	95
	Balance c/d	1,175	(9)	Drawings	1,950
		4,675			4,675
				Balance b/d	1,175

Equipment (cost)

		£		£
(1)	Bank	1,500	Balance c/d	1,500
	Balance b/d	1,500		

Accumulated depreciation

	£		£
Balance c/d	150	(12) Depreciation charge	150
		Balance b/d	150

Depreciation charge

	£		£
(12) Accumulated d'ciation	150	T/R Profit and loss	150

Rent

	£		£
(2) Capital introduced	300	T/R Profit and loss	300

Cost of Materials

		£		£
(3)	Capital introduced	50	(13) Stock	80
(6)	Trade creditors	700	T/R Profit and loss	670
		750		750

Wages

	£		£
(4) Bank	600	T/R Profit and loss	600

Insurance

	£		£
(5) Bank	30	(10) Prepayments	10
		T/R Profit and loss	20
	30		30

Electricity

	£		£
(8) Bank	95	T/R Profit and loss	120
(11) Accrued liabilities	25		
	120		120

Fees earned

	£		£
T/R Profit and loss	4,000	(7) Debtors	4,000

Stocks

	£		£
(13) Cost of materials	80	Balance c/d	80
Balance b/d	80		

Trade creditors

	£		£
(6) Bank	500	(6) Cost of materials	700
Balance c/d	200		
	700		700
		Balance b/d	200

Accrued liabilities

	£		£
Balance c/d	25	(11) Electricity	25
		Balance b/d	25

Debtors

	£			£
(7) Fees earned	4,000	(7)	Bank	3,500
			Balance c/d	500
	4,000			4,000
Balance b/d	500			

Prepayments

	£		£
(10) Insurance	10	Balance c/d	10
Balance b/d	10		

Capital introduced

	£			£
T/R Proprietor's capital	350	(2)	Rent	300
		(3)	Cost of materials	50
	350			350

Drawings

	£		£
(9) Bank	1,950	T/R Proprietor's capital	1,950

Profit and loss account

	£		£
T/R Depreciation charge	150	T/R Fees earned	4,000
T/R Rent	300		
T/R Cost of materials	670		
T/R Wages	600		
T/R Insurance	20		
T/R Electricity	120		
T/R Proprietor's capital	2,140		
	4,000		4,000

Proprietor's capital account

	£		£
T/R Drawings	1,950	T/R Capital introduced	350
Balance c/d	540	T/R Profit and loss	2,140
	2,490		2,490
		Balance b/d	540

The trial balance, taken before transfers to profit and loss and proprietor's capital, is as follows:

	Dr.	Cr.
Bank		1,175
Equipment (cost)	1,500	
Accumulated depreciation		150
Depreciation charge	150	
Rent	300	
Cost of materials	670	
Wages	600	
Insurance	20	
Electricity	120	
Fees earned		4,000
Stocks	80	
Trade creditors		200
Accrued liabilities		25
Debtors	500	
Prepayments	10	
Capital introduced		350
Drawings	1,950	
	£5,900	£5,900

The trial balance, after making transfers to the profit and loss account, consists of the balances which are brought down after balancing off each account:

	Dr.	Cr.
Bank		1,175
Equipment (cost)	1,500	
Accumulated depreciation		150
Stocks	80	
Trade creditors		200
Accrued liabilities		25
Debtors	500	
Prepayments	10	
Proprietor's capital		540
	£2,090	£2,090

This provides the data from which the closing balance sheet can be assembled: the detail of the proprietor's capital account is obtained from the account in the ledger.

Dr Seatham Rythe
Balance sheet
as at (end of period)

	£	£	£
Fixed assets			
Equipment (cost)		1,500	
Less accumulated depreciation		150	
			1,350
Current assets			
Stocks	80		
Debtors and prepayments	510		
		590	
Less current liabilities			
Trade creditors and accrued liabilities	225		
Bank overdraft	1,175		
		1,400	
Net current assets			(810)[7]
Net assets			540

Financed by:	£	£
Proprietor's capital		
Capital introduced	350	
Add income for the period	2,140	
	2,490	
Less drawings for the period	1,950	
Closing balance		540

The income statement (as the profit and loss account might be described in this case) can be obtained by rearranging the details of the profit and loss account which appeared in the ledger:

Dr Seatham Rythe
Income statement
for the period (   )

	£	£
Fees earned		4,000
Less: Expenses		
Materials	670	
Wages	600	
Electricity	120	
Depreciation	150	
Insurance	20	
Rent	300	
		1,860
Net income for the period		2,140

It is appropriate to describe the 'bottom line', in this case, as 'income' rather than 'profit' because it will substantially represent a reward for Dr Seatham Rythe's labour and skill, rather than a return on financial capital.[8] The expenses are not subdivided into direct costs (deducted in arriving at gross profit) and indirect costs (deducted in arriving at net profit) because this would not reflect the economic nature of the business. The main direct cost in economic terms is, in this case, the proprietor's own labour, which, as we have just seen, is not charged as an expense, and it is difficult to arrive at a useful subdivision of those expenses which are charged, e.g., are we to regard the receptionist as an overhead or as a direct part of the service? This illustrates the important point that we should always, within their natural constraints, design accounts in such a way that they give a 'true and fair view', reflecting economic reality as closely as possible.

The final statement which we have not yet derived is the flow of funds statement. This, it will be recalled, is derived by comparing closing balance sheet figures with the corresponding figures in the opening balance sheet. In this particular case, the opening balance sheet (before transaction (1)) was non-existent, as the business did not exist. However, looking at the closing balance sheet as a series of flows over the year and analysing the components can still be illuminating. Moreover, a flow of funds statement in this example will enable us to learn more about the fundamental properties of depreciation charges.

Looking at the closing balance sheet and bearing in mind that the initial balances were all zero gives us the following list of sources and uses of funds:

Item	Source £	Use £
Equipment (cost)		1,500
Depreciation	150	
Stocks		80
Debtors and prepayments		510
Trade creditors and accrued liabilities	225	
Bank overdraft	1,175	
Capital introduced	350	
Net income for the period	2,140	
Drawings for the period		1,950
Total	4,040	4,040

The one item in this list which is likely to be difficult to understand is depreciation. Logically the increase in depreciation must be a source of funds because it is opposite in sign (or in debit and credit terms) to the increase in the asset which is a use of funds. Intuitively, this may be difficult to understand because depreciation is thought of as a loss in value rather than a source of funds. However, we must remember how the depreciation charge was made: it was transferred out of profit (by debiting an expense, the depreciation charge) into a provision (accumulated depreciation), and this transfer did not involve any corresponding transaction with the outside world. Hence, charging depreciation against profit did not diminish the funds available to the firm, but rather put those funds into a different category. Hence it is customary to *add back* the depreciation charge to profit in order to calculate funds generated by operations.[9] It may be thought that this means that fixed assets are not a burden on the firm's funds, but this view would be incorrect, because the *cost* of the fixed asset is indeed charged as a use of funds at the time of purchase. The funds subsequently generated from operations (including the allocation to depreciation) are the compensating return on the initial outlay.

Apart from the discussion of depreciation, the only other necessary prelude to rearranging the information as a sources and uses of funds statement is to consider the precise grouping of the items. In the particular activity under consideration, the current assets and liabilities are individually quite small, and it might therefore be appropriate to group together debtors, stocks and creditors to show an increase in net working capital of £365 (made up of £510 + £80 − £225). Equally, the proprietor already has details (in the capital account) of his drawings and capital introduced, so it may be convenient here to summarise these transactions as net drawings of £1,600 (i.e., £1,950 − £350). Of the remaining items, the bank overdraft is clearly bearing the residual weight of funding this business, so that it will be appropriate to show it as the 'bottom line' balancing item, although it is stressed that this is a *funds* flow, not a *cash* flow statement.

The flow of funds statement for presentation to the proprietor might then be as follows (see next page).

This statement highlights the importance of bank borrowing, and of the equipment purchase. If no more equipment is needed in the future, Dr Rythe can look forward to a period of consolidation in which he pays off his overdraft, and in which his income may build up as his practice expands. This statement demonstrates the importance of looking at other information in conjunction with that given in the financial statements: other existing circumstances (e.g., the nature of the business and the fact that it has just started) and future prospects are often crucial in determining our interpretation of the financial record.

Dr Seatham Rythe
Flow of funds statement
for the period ( )

Sources of funds	£	£
Net income for the period	2,140	
Add increase in depreciation provision	150	
		2,290
Uses of funds		
Purchase of equipment	1,500	
Net drawings by the proprietor	1,600	
Increase in net working capital	365	
		3,465
Less increase in bank overdraft		1,175
		2,290

REVIEW, AND PLAN OF THE REMAINING CHAPTERS

This chapter has completed the discussion of the basic accounting framework. We have now analysed the elements of financial statements and their derivation from double entry accounting records. However, we have concentrated on technique rather than interpretation, and the next chapter will discuss the elements of interpretation of financial statements. Such a discussion cannot be complete without consideration of the limitations of an accounting system based on historical cost, and so the following chapter will discuss valuation, price changes and inflation accounting. We shall then return briefly to a discussion of further aspects of accounting systems, because our illustration of the double entry system has concentrated on the logical essentials, at the expense of some other features which are important in practice. Finally, the last chapter of the book will suggest further reading and provide thumbnail sketches of interesting aspects of accounting which we have had to ignore within the confines of an elementary introductory text.

George Square had the following balances in his books at 1 January 19__

George Square
Trial balance at 1 January 19..

	Dr.	Cr.
Trade creditors		2,300
Stocks of raw materials	1,200	
Work-in-progress	1,400	
Stocks of finished goods	700	
Machinery, at cost	2,500	
Accumulated depreciation		500
Bank overdraft		1,250
Trade debtors	1,500	
Proprietor's capital		3,250
	£7,300	£7,300

His transactions during the year are shown below.

(All cash transactions are conducted by means of the bank account.)

(All factory costs with the exception of depreciation are assumed to add to the value of work-in-progress.)

1   Bought office premises for £4,000 by means of a long-term mortgage loan, at 10 per cent per annum interest.
2   Spent £3,000 on raw materials. He paid £2,200 by cheque and bought the remainder on credit.
3   Paid wages of £4,000 of which £1,500 was for office staff and the remainder for direct factory labour.
4   Materials costing £2,700 were used in production.
5   Work-in-progress costing £3,000 was transferred to finished goods.
6   Rent on the factory premises of £300 was paid.
7   George Square took £400 as drawings during the course of the year.
8   Insurance on the office and factory machinery of £600 was paid (two–thirds of the insurance was for office premises).
9   £900 was paid for electricity and a further £100 was outstanding at the end of the year. (Three quarters of the electricity is used in the factory.)
10   Finished goods costing £2,500 were sold on credit for £6,000. £7,000 was received from debtors during the year.
11   The machinery is to be depreciated at the rate of £250 p.a. and the office premises at the rate of £500 p.a.
12   Paid interest for the year on the mortgage loan.

Required

(a) To write up George Square's ledger for the year, including separate accounts for various expenses and sources of revenue.

(b) As you write up the ledger, record in journal form how you deal with each transaction.

(c) Prove your work by drawing up a trial balance at the end of the year.

(d) Produce a trading and profit and loss account, balance sheet and flow of funds statement. (The profit and loss account and balance sheet may be in either vertical or horizontal format, and the flow of funds statement may highlight either the change in the cash position, or the change in working capital.)

(e) What is your assessment of the performance of George Square's business during the year? (This may be deferred until chapter 6 has been read, but it might be useful to give some thought to the subject before reading the chapter.)

THE INTERPRETATION OF ACCOUNTS

INTRODUCTION

It is usual, in introductory accounting texts, to have a chapter on the interpretation of accounts. This typically concentrates on the description, detailed definition and computation of various accounting ratios.

The interpretation of accounts is undoubtedly important. Indeed, it is crucial: there is no point in spending resources preparing accounts if we cannot interpret them. Equally, ratios can and do play an important part in the interpretation of accounts. However, just as concentration on the techniques of assembling accounting data can distract attention from restrictive assumptions implicit in the process (such as the historic cost assumption, which we have adopted hitherto but will be questioned in the next chapter), so also can an excessive concentration on the computation of ratios distract attention from some of the fundamental issues in the interpretation of accounts. For this reason, we shall concentrate first on a discussion of fundamental issues followed by a discussion of the principles of ratio analysis and an outline of the broad categories of ratios which are commonly used, rather than their computational details.

The fundamental issues which will be discussed are as follows:

(1) Definition of the *purpose* of interpretation is essential.
(2) Accounting data are usually interpreted in the context of *other information*.
(3) Accounts are a *system*, so that individual accounting ratios can rarely be interpreted independently of others.
(4) Accounting *data are imperfect*, and their interpretation must allow for this.

DEFINITION OF THE PURPOSE

A good answer requires a good question. To see this, the reader need only be reminded of the extreme example in *The Hitchhiker's Guide to the Galaxy*[1] in which a powerful computer (Deep Thought) spends millions of years finding the answer to the Ultimate Question. When the answer (42) is finally obtained, it is of no use because nobody knows the Ultimate Question.

When interpreting financial information we need to be clear about what we want and *why* we want to know it. The 'want' will not usually take the form of 'What is the ratio of gross profit to sales?', but a rather more general question, such as 'Is this a profitable firm?'. Thus, we are likely to use a variety of information, rather than a single number, and the selection of information will, in part, be a matter of judgement. The 'why' implies a particular purpose. In exercising judgement to select information, we must have some knowledge as to the purpose for which it is to be used. For example, is it to evaluate past performance or to estimate prospects for the future?

This leads us to a third aspect of interpretation'. '*Who* is the user of the financial information?' It is necessary to know this, because different users will have different perspectives. A shareholder, for example, will be interested in the future prospects for increasing dividends, whereas a creditor, who has no prospect of participating in higher future returns, may be merely interested in the firm's ability to meet its liabilities. Sometimes, the different perspectives may lead to directly contradictory views of information: an increase in the wage bill is, *prima facie*, good news from the point of view of employees (indicating more employment or higher rates of pay) but bad from the point of view of shareholders (whose profits are thereby reduced). The 'who' question may also affect the degree of sophistication appropriate to the interpretation: the degree of technical detail which might be useful to a professional investment analyst might not be useful, and might even be confusing, to an ordinary small shareholder.

OTHER INFORMATION

The performance or financial position of a firm (or part of a firm) has to be looked at in its economic context. For example, modest profits in hard times can indicate a more creditable performance than higher profits in more prosperous times. The same applies to industry or activity: moderate profitability might indicate the best performance in a declining industry or the worst in a prosperous industry. Moreover, accounts are based primarily on past transactions and present assets and claims, whereas many uses of accounts are concerned with the future. In assessing the future, we must take a view as to the likely state of the economic environment in which the firm operates and the firm's position within that environment, e.g., which markets it sells in and obtains its factors of production from.

In assessing the state of the firm itself, there is much relevant information about the firm which does not appear in the main accounts but may appear by way of a note or, in the case of a company, in the Directors' Report or the Chairman's Statement. For example, the firm may have undergone a re-structuring process, which has temporarily depressed reported profits or other performance measures, but will improve future performance. Changes of senior management may also be important, as will be take-overs and mergers, which not only affect future performance but can have considerable distortionary effects on the way in which the accounts reflect performance: take-overs and mergers are a fruitful area for the creative accountant. A particularly useful source of information can be the Chairman's Statement, which usually reviews recent performance, outlines current plans and some-times even gives informal forecasts. This statement is not audited or regulated by accounting standards, and this makes it a useful vehicle for 'soft' information which, although not very reliable, may be highly relevant to the user's assessment of the company.

Another source of company-specific information comes from stockbrokers and other analysts who visit companies listed on the stock exchange and investigate their current state and future plans. This relationship is restrained by 'insider trading' rules, which forbid the use in the stock market of information which is not publicly available. If rules of this type did not exist, senior managers of companies, who have access to privileged, price-sensitive information, could profit greatly, at the expense of other shareholders, by acting upon it. For this reason, great care is taken that information about such matters as interim or annual profits, dividends, take-over offers or major new contracts is made public in a prompt and systematic way, so that the alert shareholder who uses public information sources should be able to trade on the basis of the best available current information.

There are, of course, many sources of information relating to the economic environment which are not company-specific but which will affect the assessment of different companies in different ways, e.g., a rise in the price of crude oil is likely to affect the profits of oil companies, and those which produce relatively more crude oil 'upstream' rather than refining and retailing 'downstream' are likely to be the beneficiaries. Equally, an increase in interest rates will put a relatively high immediate burden on companies which are heavy short-term borrowers, and fluctuations in exchange rates will affect exporters and importers in different ways. It is the importance of such factors as these which have led large investment institutions to employ more economists in recent years, in the hope of improving their forecasts and of giving a better understanding of the impact of economic events on the prospects of specific firms or industries.

ACCOUNTS AS A SYSTEM

The most important questions which require the interpretation of accounts are far from simple (e.g. Should I sell my shares? Can the company afford a pay rise? Should I lend to the company?). They involve a number of aspects of the firm's performance, e.g., a lender is likely to be interested both in profitability and in liquidity as indicators of the firm's ability to pay interest and redeem the loan, and, as the ultimate defence, may also be interested in the amount of assets available to repay the loan if the firm is forced into liquidation.[2]

For this reason, the interpretation of accounts usually involves looking at the accounts, and therefore the firm, as a system, rather than merely considering a single aspect in isolation. In this process, particular accounting measures may take on a different significance in different contexts. For example, liquidity measures are often listed as an important element in standard ratio analysis of accounts, but a 'poor' liquidity ratio (e.g., a low ratio of current assets to current liabilities) may have little significance in the context of a highly profitable firm which is able either to borrow more or raise more equity capital.

It is therefore most important, before launching into detailed ratio analysis, to define the question clearly and to consider how it might best be answered by drawing from the full accounting system described earlier (chapter 2). It will be recalled that this consisted of a balance sheet which showed the financial position at a point of time, a flow of funds statement indicating the flows leading to changes in the composition of the balance sheet over a period and a profit and loss account which amplified the composition of a particularly important flow, the profit or loss achieved over a period. All of these statements are related to one another, and the relationship is one of interpretive significance, not merely a matter of arithmetic.

IMPERFECTIONS OF ACCOUNTING INFORMATION

It should be apparent from the discussion in earlier chapters that accounting data are imperfect in many ways. One of the more obvious of these is the valuation basis used, which often is calculated on a historical basis (what was paid for an asset or received for a liability) rather than a current basis (what values to attach to those assets or liabilities in the market at the present time). This is part of the more general problem that financial accounts tend to report transactions *ex post*, whereas the user of accounts is often more interested in the present financial position and future prospects of the business.

We shall discuss in the next chapter some possible ways of dealing with changing prices in accounts, but, although this might improve the informational value of accounts, neither adjusting for changing prices nor changing the whole orientation of financial accounts from the past to the future would eliminate entirely the imperfections of accounting data. A basic reason for this is that uncertainty pervades accounting measurement, reflecting the uncertainty which necessarily surrounds business decisions. By moving the emphasis of accounts from the less relevant past to the more relevant future, we are likely to increase the element of uncertainty, because the past has at least a firm record of completed transactions whereas the future is necessarily a matter of probabilities rather than certainties. Thus, we trade greater 'softness' of information for greater relevance.

Apart from the trade-off between reliability and relevance, the 'all purpose' nature of financial accounts means that they necessarily represent a compromise between the needs of different users and classes of user. Thus, some users may require information which is above all objective (e.g., when the accounts are used as the basis of a legal contract, such as a loan contract or an employee bonus contract) whereas others may be willing to sacrifice objectivity for relevance (e.g., purchasers of equity shares, who are essentially taking on the residual risk of a company). Also different users may have different information requirements, even when the use is similar, e.g., there has been much discussion of simplified accounts for small shareholders who may not have the analytical skills necessary to use a complex set of accounts which disclose the high level of information which may (or may not) be of use to the skilled investment analyst. It is unlikely that one set of accounts will be able to provide information which will meet ideally the needs of all these users and uses.

SOME BASIC ASPECTS OF RATIO ANALYSIS

Having stressed the important broad principles which must be borne in mind when analysing accounts, we can consider basic ratio analysis, hopefully without the danger that a ritual of calculating ratios will become a substitute for sensible analytical thought.

Ratio analysis is widely used in practice and is in many ways a natural way to look at accounting data. The reason for this is that we often wish to use the data for *comparative* purposes, either between firms at the same time, or between the same firm at different times. Different firms will be of different sizes, and the same firm will be of different sizes at different times (especially in periods of changing prices) and we must remove the size effect if comparisons are to be meaningful, e.g., total debt of £1 million might be considered large for a firm with total assets of only £1½ million, but small for a firm with assets of £100 million. A ratio with size as the denominator, is a natural means of removing the size effect: in this example, we could calculate a debt/assets ratio of $\frac{2}{3}$ for the first firm and $\frac{1}{100}$ for the second. The size measure needs to be selected with some care as being appropriate to the question being asked (most firms are of different sizes in different components of their accounts), and in the case of debt it is usual to relate it to proprietors' net worth to give a gearing (in the UK) or leverage (in the USA) ratio.

An alternative use of ratios is to treat them as representing causal relationships from the denominator to the numerator, e.g., we might interpret a ratio of gross profit to sales as indicating that sales create gross profits. If we assume that this ratio is constant, we can use it for predictive purposes, e.g., if it is expected that sales will increase by a quarter we would expect gross profit to increase by the same proportion. However, this involves very strong assumptions. Not only are we assuming that the relationship between sales and gross profit is constant, but, by putting it in ratio firm, we are assuming that it is a linear, proportionate relationship, as portrayed in (a) below:

(a) A linear proportionate (ratio) relationship

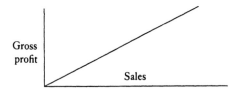

There are two plausible sources of violation of this assumption. Firstly, there might be a source of gross profit which is not dependent on sales, so that there is a constant term in the relationship, as in (b) below:

(b) A linear relationship with a constant term

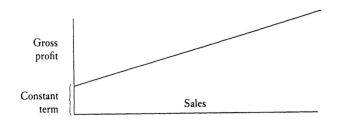

More plausibly, the linearity assumption might be violated, e.g., because increasing sales were the result of keener pricing and lower profit margins. The latter would lead to the type of relationship shown in (c) below:

(c) A non-linear relationship

Thus, ratios are potentially misleading as predictive devices and are, at best, likely to be approximations. For this reason, the remainder of our discussion will focus on ratios as a means of comparison, rather than prediction.

SOME KEY RATIOS

The interpretation of accounts in general, and the use of ratios in particular, usually focus on three key areas: profitability, liquidity and financial structure. We shall deal with each in turn, although previous warnings about the interdependence of different aspects, and the limitations of accounting data, must be borne in mind.

Profitability

We usually measure profitability in terms of the ratio:

$$\frac{\text{Profits}}{\text{Assets employed}}$$

The ratio is thus designed to show the effectiveness with which assets are used in generating profits. Apart from the obvious limitations of accounting measurement, some more precise definitional problems deserve mention.

Firstly, profits must be defined for the particular purpose which we have in mind: gross profit may be used as a measure of trading and operating success, and net profit (after deducting overhead costs) as a measure of overall success. Net profit before deducting interest payments may be relevant to loan stock holders (long-term lenders to companies), who wish to see the 'cover' for their interest payments, but net profit after interest payments may be of more interest to proprietors (or shareholders in companies) whose claims are limited to this measure of profit.

Having defined profit, we need to define assets in such a way as to be consistent with it. Thus, profit before interest payments should be related to a measure of net assets which includes interest bearing liabilities (i.e., proprietors' net worth *plus* interest-bearing liabilities), whereas profit after interest payments should be related to proprietors' (or shareholders') net worth. Another small, but potentially important aspect of asset measurement is that assets are measured at a point in time, whereas profit is measured over a *period* of time. Thus, we should ideally like to relate profit to *average* assets employed, not closing assets (as appearing in the closing balance sheet which accompanies the profit and loss account) or opening assets. An approximation to average assets which is often used and may be useful is to average opening and closing assets. This can be misleading when there is a large discrete jump in assets employed, e.g., due to a take-over ... but take-overs involve many other potential pitfalls for the interpreter of accounts.[3]

A potentially useful decomposition of profitability is the following identity:

$$\frac{\text{Profit}}{\text{Assets}} \equiv \frac{\text{Profit}}{\text{Sales}} \times \frac{\text{Sales}}{\text{Assets}}$$

In some circumstances, it may be useful to distinguish the effects on profitability of a change in the margin on sales (the profit/sales ratio) from the effects of a change in the rate of activity (the sales/assets ratio). These effects may sometimes reinforce one another (e.g., when the sales and profit margin are both rising in response to an increase in demand), and at other times they may work in opposite directions (e.g., when prices, and therefore profit margins, are cut to increase sales, when other factors have not increased demand).

Liquidity

Liquidity is the degree to which a firm's potential access to cash covers its debts. It is important for the survival of a firm. A firm which becomes extremely illiquid becomes insolvent, i.e., unable to pay its debts as and when they become due, and may be driven into liquidation (if it is a company) or bankruptcy of the proprietors (if it is unincorporated). These legal processes may involve selling up the firm's assets (and those of proprietors not protected by limited liability), the proceeds being applied to the creditors. This situation is undesirable from the point of view of both proprietors (who often lose their stake in the business) and creditors (who receive payments later and, often, only in part.)

It is important to remember that, except in the extreme case in which the firm is currently unable to pay its debts (in which case we do not need to predict failure, because it has already occurred), the assessment of liquidity depends upon estimating future events. These events are potential cash flows which may be derived not only from currently held assets which appear in the balance sheet (e.g., trade debtors) but also from future operations of the firm (i.e., cash from sales, less cash cost of sales) and from future borrowing or other sources of finance. Future profitability will be important in assessing the latter prospects, and the analysis of flow funds and cash flow statements may also be helpful. This reinforces the warning given earlier that we must look at the accounts as a system and not become too reliant on a limited number of narrow measures.

However, there are a number of commonly used liquidity ratios which are of assistance in assessing liquidity, and how it has changed, even if they provide only part of the picture and must be complemented by further investigation. The latest balance sheet, which lists assets and claims in order of their liquidity, is the natural place to start an

assessment of the current state of the firm, and one obvious measure is
the current asset ratio:

$$\frac{\text{Current assets}}{\text{Current liabilities}}$$

Clearly, if this ratio is less than one, when all existing current assets and
liabilities have matured, the proceeds of the assets will be inadequate to
pay off the liabilities, so that there must be a prospect of a net cash
inflow from other sources, if the firm is to avoid insolvency. However,
current assets typically include stocks and work-in-progress, which the
firm must continue to hold (or replace) if it is to remain in business and
which may not be readily saleable even in those cases in which the firm
would not wish to replace them. This suggests a narrower definition of
liquid (rather than current) assets, and the corresponding liquid asset
ratio:

$$\frac{(\text{Current assets} - \text{stocks})}{\text{Current liabilities}}$$

In using ratios to diagnose the liquidity of the firm, we might wish to
probe deeper by examining some ratios relating to components of liquid
assets. By relating these to sales (which is sometimes misleadingly
referred to as turnover) we can obtain insights into some important
aspects of current operations. For example, it is necessary for the firm
to allow credit to its customers (trade debtors) in many trades and a firm
which is not very efficient at collecting its debts or has unreliable
debtors (potential 'bad debts' which will never be paid off) or is finding
it difficult to sell its product (credit being one way of encouraging
customers to buy) will tend to have a larger debtor/sales ratio:

$$\frac{\text{Trade debtors}}{\text{Sales}}$$

Sales are normally measured over a year and debtors as at the end of the
year. To obtain the average credit period in weeks, we multiply this ratio
by fifty-two. It must be remembered that closing debtors may not be
typical of the firm's position, either because the business is seasonal or
because the firm has deliberately 'window-dressed' its balance sheet by
collecting an unusual proportion of debts at the balance sheet date.

An analogous ratio showing the credit period which the firm obtains from its creditors is the creditor/purchases ratio:

$$\frac{\text{Trade creditors}}{\text{Purchases}}$$

Sometimes, the purchases figure may not be available from published accounts and it may be necessary to use the cruder cost of sales measure as a substitute: this may include components such as wages which do not usually carry a significant credit element. As with the debtor/sales ratio, we can translate this ratio into a weekly credit period by multiplying by fifty-two. A relatively high creditor/purchases ratio can be a good thing, if it implies that the firm is given large amounts of free credit willingly by its suppliers. However, if the credit period is stretched to its limit, discounts can be lost and suppliers may either raise prices or refuse to supply.

A third ratio of this type is the stock turnover ratio:

$$\frac{\text{Cost of sales}}{\text{Stock}}$$

This tells us how many times existing stock would be expected to 'turn over' during the period, e.g., if stock costing £1.2 million (cost of sales) is produced during the year and stocks costing £100,000 are held at the year end, annual production is twelve times stock, so we would expect stock to be replaced twelve times during the year. The inverse of this ratio is the stock holding period: one month ($\frac{1}{12} \times 12$) in our example. The higher is stock turnover (or the lower the stock holding period) the less capital is tied up in stocks. This may also be taken as an indicator of the strength of demand, although extremely low stock levels can lead to supply failures (through 'stockouts' occurring) and, ultimately, loss of business. Like the two credit ratios, the stock ratios are vulnerable to 'window-dressing' of the closing balance sheet.

Capital structure

Long-term investors in a firm are often assumed to be the primary users of financial statements. These users will be interested in the security of their investment and the associated returns. Two primary ratios of this type are the gearing ratio and the retention ratio.

Gearing (or, in the USA, leverage) is the extent to which the long-term funds of a firm are provided on a fixed interest basis. This is important because fixed interest carries a legal obligation to pay and can lead to the firm becoming insolvent if it is unable to pay. Thus, lenders do not like the gearing ratio to become too high because it increases the risk that, if profits fall, their interest payments may not be met and their capital will be at risk. Thus, long-term lenders may insist that the firm enter into debt covenants, which restrict further fixed interest borrowing beyond a level of gearing which might put their investment at risk. Long-term borrowing has become increasingly important in recent years, and much recent effort in creative accounting has been devoted to making the gearing ratio look lower, in order to allow further borrowing or to reduce possible anxieties about the existing level of borrowing.

Gearing is commonly measured in two separate ways, in balance sheet terms and in profit and loss terms. The balance sheet measure of gearing is:

$$\frac{\text{Long-term loans}}{\text{Proprietors' net worth}}$$

In a company, shareholders' funds would be substituted for proprietors' net worth, in the denominator. The numerator can present difficulties in companies because of the existence of preference shares: these are shares which carry a preferential fixed dividend, subject to a profit being available. Thus, although they carry a prior claim over ordinary shares when distributing dividends, the discretionary nature of the dividend means that they cannot drive the company into insolvency in the same way as interest-bearing debts. This suggests that, insofar as the gearing measure is used as a measure of financial risk (i.e., risk created by the firm's financial structure), preference shares should not be regarded as part of gearing but rather as shareholders' funds.

The balance sheet measure of gearing represents gearing at a particular point in time and, furthermore, is subject to the well-known limitations of balance sheet valuations. For example, the balance sheet value of fixed-interest loans is the nominal value (i.e., the amount at which the loan is ultimately redeemable) rather than the current market value. An alternative method of calculating gearing is in terms of the profit and loss account:

$$\frac{\text{Fixed interest payments for the period}}{\text{Profit for the period}}$$

This shows the proportion of profit which is taken up by the fixed interest payments and therefore shows the extent to which current profit covers those payments: clearly, the higher the ratio, the less secure are interest payments. From the shareholders' point of view, this ratio gives some indication of the sensitivity to pre-interest profits of the shareholders' residual profit share: high gearing means a high return to an increase in pre-interest profits and a high loss to a decrease, from the shareholders' point of view. If we wish to separate out the ordinary shareholders' point of view and we are interested in future profit shares rather than financial security, it might be appropriate to include preference dividends with interest payments in the numerator. This income-based measure of gearing is also subject to the problems of measurement, since the measurement of profit depends upon the valuation and capital maintenance policies used in the accounts: these problems will be discussed further in the next chapter.

The other key measure of financial structure is the retention ratio. This shows the proportion of the net profits, usually after all expenses (including interest) and taxation, which is retained in the business rather than distributed to the proprietors. In a company, this is:

$$\frac{\text{Retained profits}}{\text{Profits available for ordinary shareholders}}$$

In an unincorporated business, the denominator would be profits available for distribution to proprietors. This ratio shows us two things. Firstly, it shows the extent to which the business is ploughing back profits to strengthen its future position. If the rate of return on proprietors' (or shareholders') net worth remains constant, for example, we can assume that future profits will be increased in proportion to the growth by retention, which is obtained from the following identity:

$$\frac{\text{Retentions}}{\text{Profit}} \times \frac{\text{Profit}}{\text{Net worth}} = \frac{\text{Retentions}}{\text{Net worth}}$$

This assumes that all of the elements are defined consistently, in terms of post-tax profits attributable to shareholders (or proprietors) and net worth attributable to the same group. Multiplying the retention ratio by the current rate of profit gives proportionate growth of net worth by retention (on the right-hand side). If the profit rate remains constant in future, profit will grow in the same proportion as a result of retention, although many other factors are also likely to affect future profits (e.g., costs, demand and investment financed from sources other than retention).

A second use of the retention ratio is to show the 'cover' for the dividend in a company. From the ordinary shareholders' point of view, the higher the ratio, the better the cover (e.g., a value of one half indicates that retentions are equal to distributions) and the better the prospect that dividends can be maintained or increased in the future. An alternative way of calculating dividend cover is:

$$\frac{\text{Profits available for dividends}}{\text{Dividends}}$$

This is a 'times covered' ratio, which shows exactly how many times current dividends are covered by current profits (although tax can introduce complications into this calculation, in practice). A similar ratio can be calculated for interest payments, as an alternative to the profit and loss account measure of gearing discussed earlier.

Finally, there are certain ratios which are important in the evaluation of companies whose shares are listed on a stock exchange, so that a market price is available. The most basic is perhaps earnings per share:

$$\frac{\text{Earnings available for ordinary shareholders}}{\text{Number of shares}}$$

This can be calculated for any company, but it is particularly important when the shares are regularly appraised in the market place. It is only a starting point, because it tells us *current* earnings (or earnings in the latest accounts), whereas the investor is interested in future earnings (which are the source of future dividends or gains in share price) and in the degree of risk surrounding them. The investor is also interested in how expensive the share is to buy, i.e., what does it cost to gain a share of this earnings stream? For this purpose, we may use earnings yield:

$$\frac{\text{Earnings per share}}{\text{Price per share}}$$

or the more popular inverse of this, the price/earnings ratio:

$$P/E = \frac{\text{Price per share}}{\text{Earnings per share}}$$

The higher the P/E ratio, the more expensive are current earnings, indicating that the market believes them to be of higher quality in terms of future growth prospects or immunity from risk.[4]

The shareholder who has a particular interest in immediate cash returns may wish to look at the dividend yield:

$$\frac{\text{Dividend per share}}{\text{Price per share}}$$

The higher the dividend yield, the higher will be immediate returns, but dividends in the longer term are likely to depend on future earnings more than on current dividend levels.

CONCLUSION

We have very briefly surveyed a number of ratios which are commonly used in the analysis of accounts. More detailed, but still elementary, treatment of accounting ratios, with practical examples of their computation will be found in the books by Bird and Rutherford (1989) and Parker (1988). The best advanced text on financial statement analysis is probably Foster (1986). All of these are strongly recommended for further reading (see chapter 9).

The warnings given earlier in the chapter must now be reiterated. It is potentially very misleading to concentrate on a limited range of financial ratios: the accounts must be analysed as a system. Moreover, that system must be viewed in the context of a wider information system of qualitative and quantitative information about factors which will affect a company's present position and future performance and which is available from sources other than accounts. Finally, the accounts themselves are subject to serious potential measurement errors. One important source of such errors is explored in the next chapter, which deals with accounting for changing prices.

EXERCISES

(1) Provide a brief assessment of the performance of George Square's business, as recorded in the exercise to chapter 5.

(2)   The following exercise revises techniques learned in earlier chapters
and asks for discussion of the relevance of the accounts to particular
problems, rather than detailed ratio analysis.

You have just received a legacy from your late uncle with which you have
purchased a tennis court and pavilion and have started a private tennis club.
Listed below are the transactions in your first year of trading. You are *required* to
record these in a double entry system. Prove your work by drawing up a trial
balance and your closing balance sheet. Calculate your profit for the year and
arrange the profit and loss account in a form which would reveal which aspect of
your business appeared to be most profitable. Discuss any problems which may
arise in determining the overall profit or loss and in judging the most profitable
area.

1   You purchase with your own money the court and the pavilion for
£3,000.
2   As the pavilion has been derelict for two years, you pay £500 with your
own money on repairs to make the structure sound.
3   You purchase, on credit, £1,000 of bar fittings and equipment.
4   100 members join the club, each paying £20 cash, which entitles them to
use the tennis court and pavilion facilities for one year.
5   You pay £500 cash for wines and spirits.
6   Wines and spirits sold during the year amount to £1,850 (cash) (cost
price £400).
7   Groundsman's wages amount to £1,250 (cash).
8   Part-time barman's wages total £250 (cash).
9   You draw out £300 cash to pay rates on your own house.
10   Food for the restaurant costs £500, of which £300 is paid in cash and
£200 is still owing. No food stock remained at the end of the period.
11   Catering wages amount to £450 (cash).
12   Restaurant takings amount to £1,600.

Chapter 7

ACCOUNTING FOR
PRICE CHANGES

INTRODUCTION

Hitherto, we have illustrated the basic financial statements and the underlying system of double entry book-keeping by using the historical cost method of measurement. This method was chosen because it is the one which has been preferred traditionally by accountants and which is most commonly found in practice. However, the pace of changing prices has, in recent years, called into question the relevance of historical costs as a basis for reporting on the current state and performance of a business, and the historical cost convention has been increasingly eroded, e.g., in the UK many companies practise piecemeal revaluation of certain fixed assets and in certain Latin American countries there are requirements for accounts to be prepared on an inflation-adjusted basis (broadly of the type described as CPP (constant purchasing power) in this chapter). This chapter outlines the main methods which are available for incorporating price changes into accounts. This should be useful for two purposes. Firstly, to give the reader some insight into the accounting problems caused by changing prices and the means by which they might be dealt with. Secondly, the methods of price change accounting provide a useful technical exercise in double entry accounting, which should give the reader further insight into the properties of the accounting framework described in earlier chapters.

Despite persistent warnings that historical costs do not represent current values and may therefore be irrelevant to the current state of the business, the first five chapters of this book should have demonstrated why historical cost is in many ways a method which appeals naturally to accountants. It is transaction-based, and therefore enters the recording process naturally and objectively at the time of purchase. Subsequent adjustments to acquisition cost, other than caused by disposal (another transaction, establishing a new historical cost), are not forced by any particular event, are subjective and, if verified by an independent valuer, expensive. Hence, accountants have typically confined themselves to rule-of-thumb adjustments to historical cost, such as the depreciation adjustment, and have resorted to current valuation only when forced by the requirements of prudence (e.g., in the case of stocks, when market value falls below historical cost).

However, we concluded chapter 6, which dealt with the interpretation of accounts, with a statement that the traditional valuation base of accounting is often a source of measurement error. The assumption behind this statement was that users of accounts are interested in the *current* rather than the historical state of the business. They therefore would prefer to see the current values of assets and claims, rather than out-of-date historical values, in the balance sheet, and the current value of sales less the current cost of sales in the profit and loss account. The gap between current values and historical costs is particularly wide following a period of rapid price changes, and this is probably why price change accounting has always tended to become an important issue in periods of high inflation. It is notable that in the United Kingdom at the present time, despite the abandonment of fully fledged price change accounting (required by an accounting standard in 1980, but effectively abandoned in 1986), many firms are experimenting, to an increasing extent, with current valuations of certain assets and claims. This probably reflects the fact that the rate of inflation is still at a relatively high level by historical standards (although not as high as that of the 1970s, which led to pressure for a comprehensive price change accounting system), so that durable fixed assets, in particular, are typically under-valued by a significant amount if stated at historical cost.

Despite the fact that price changes are typically more important when inflation is high, it is important to distinguish between inflation and price changes. *Pure inflation* is a decline in the value of money, i.e., a proportionate increase in the money price of all other assets. Price changes relate to the money prices of *specific* assets and can therefore have two components, one attributable to general inflation (i.e., the general purchasing power of money) and the other due to the change in the price of the specific asset relative to that of other assets. *Relative price changes* can occur even when the general price level is stable, i.e., there is no inflation.[1] Thus, the problem of price change accounting can exist when there is no general inflation, because relative price changes can still occur, although general inflation (or deflation) adds a second component to price changes which may reinforce the first, to bring historical costs still further out of line with current values.

In order to illustrate the central problems of price-change accounting, we shall adopt a very simple, stylised example, which draws out the essence of what can seem to be a very complex problem. Assume that a market trader, 'Old Fred', starts the day with £100 in cash. He goes early in the morning to the wholesale market, where he buys 100 pineapples for £1 each. During the day, he sells them all for £1.50 each. Thus, at the end of the day, his historical cost profit is:

	£
Sales	150
Less historical cost of goods sold	100
historical cost profit	50

This is an objective statement of fact: he started the day with £100 in cash and ended with £150 in cash.

However, even this simple tale has a number of potential twists. Firstly, let us suppose that, at the close of business, the price of pineapples on the wholesale market had risen to £1.25 each. If Fred wanted to replace his stock of pineapples, they would now cost £125, giving the following revised profit calculation:

	£
Sales	150
Less replacement cost of goods sold	125
Current cost profit	25

This is the basis of *replacement cost* (RC) or *current cost* accounting,[3] (CCA). It shows profit after the proprietor has charged the current cost of replacing the stock of assets, or 'operating capability' of the business.

Of course, in a business like market trading, it might be inappropriate to think narrowly in terms of maintaining stocks of pineapples: why not switch to bananas or oranges if pineapples have become expensive? The same type of objection can be made, in more subtle ways, to the idea of replacing specific assets or operating capability in most types of industry. However, there is an alternative objection to the historical cost calculation: this calculation was based on the idea of profit as a surplus of closing money capital over opening money capital (by £50), as a measure of the 'better-offness' of the proprietor. If there there had been *general inflation* during the period, then £150 at the end of the period would not be worth £50 more than £100 at the beginning, because the closing £ had less purchasing power than the opening £. Suppose that inflation, as measured by a general purchasing power index, was 10 per cent during the day (indicating a state of hyper-inflation which is fortunately not common, but which simply magnifies the problems of more usual levels of inflation). If Old Fred wished to calculate his profit on an inflation-proofed, or *constant purchasing power* (CPP) basis, the result would be.[4]

	£
Sales	150
Less historical cost of goods sold, in current £'s (£100 × 1.1)	110
Constant purchasing power profit	40

Thus, we have seen that, even in a business which holds only cash in its opening and closing balance sheets, thus avoiding the valuation problem (since cash is, by definition, denominated in unambiguous cash terms), there are still three concepts of accounting profit: one based on historical money amounts determined by past transactions, one on the current cost of specific assets as determined by the market (but not confirmed by a transaction), and one on historical money amounts adjusted by subsequent changes in the general purchasing power of money. We can add to these three concepts another, which combines the second and the third and, in this case (but not in general), yields the same result as the third. This calculates profit initially on the current cost basis, to give a figure for 'operating profit', but then adds the real gain which Old Fred made by buying early (when the cost was £1) rather than later (when cost had risen to £1.25). This is sometimes described as a 'holding gain' (i.e., gain on holding assets while the market price rises), and in the present case it is a 'real' holding gain because we measure the extent to which the gain exceeded general inflation (i.e., £1.25 − (£1 × 1.1), or 15p. per unit, which amounts to £15 in aggregate). Moreover, the stock has now been sold, so that the gain is a 'realised' real holding gain.[5] The resulting profit calculation is sometimes described as the *real terms* method:

	£
Sales	150
Less current cost of goods sold	125
Current cost operating profit	25
Add real holding gain on stock	15
Real terms profit	40

THE BALANCE SHEET

In the course of this extremely simple illustration, we have ignored one of the fundamental conventions of accounting, double entry. The various adjustments were made as single entries to the profit and loss account rather than as double entries. In order to trace the double entry, we must examine the fundamental statement which gives rise to it, the balance sheet, which was also ignored in the illustration.

Old Fred's opening and closing balance sheets are remarkably simple. His opening balance sheet contained one asset, cash £100, and so did his closing balance sheet, cash £150. There were no liabilities, so that there was one aggregate claim, proprietor's capital, which was £100 at the beginning and £150 at the end. If we can assume that the £100 at the beginning represented capital newly contributed by the proprietor, rather than accumulated in the past, the opening balance sheet on any of our methods of accounting would be:

Opening balance sheet

	£		£
Proprietor's capital	100	Cash	100

Under the *historical cost* system, the closing balance sheet would be:

Closing balance sheet

	£	£		£
Proprietor's capital:			Cash	150
Opening balance	100			
Add profit for the period	50			
Closing balance		150		
		150		150

This is very straightforward and should require no elaboration.

Under the *current cost* system, our balance sheet would not balance, if we simply added CCA profit of £125 to opening capital. This is because we have not obeyed the principles of double entry. We have debited cost of sales with £25, the excess of replacement cost of stock over historical cost, but have made no credit. The credit of £25 is what we have previously described as a '*holding gain*', the difference between what we bought, as asset, and its current value (or value on disposal). This particular holding gain is measured in *money* terms, not in 'real' terms, i.e., it is the simple difference between historical cost in £'s and current cost in £'s, with no adjustment for general inflation. It is also a *realised* holding gain, since the asset has been sold. The problem which faces us is what to do with this realised holding gain, which is the missing credit in our accounting system. One approach would be to credit it to the profit and loss account as a source of revenue,[6] but that would prevent us from producing a CCA profit and loss account which showed gains from operations (in Fred's case, trading), whilst preserving enough capital (in Fred's case, pineapples) to maintain the current level of activity (operating capability). We therefore adopt the alternative of crediting the gain 'below the line' (i.e., after profit is calculated) direct to a revaluation reserve. This is an example of *reserve accounting*, which breaks the direct articulation of the reported profit figure with the change in the proprietor's net worth in the balance sheet.

Our double entry is therefore:

	Dr.	Cr.
Cost of sales	£25	
Revaluation reserve		£25

In current cost accounting, as implemented in the United Kingdom in the early 1980s, the debit to profit and loss was known as the 'cost of sales adjustment' and was reported separately from the historical cost of sales.

We can now complete our *current cost (CCA)* closing balance sheet:

Closing balance sheet

	£	£		£
Proprietor's capital				
Opening balance	100		Cash	150
Revaluation reserve	25			
	125			
Add profit for the period	25			
		150		
		150		150

The *constant purchasing power* (CPP) profit and loss account also had an adjustment to profit. This was based on a general index, to reflect pure inflation, rather than the specific index used in CCA, but the double entry implementation of the adjustment is similar to that used for CCA. The debit to profit and loss is matched by a credit to a reserve (re-statement of opening capital), as follows:

	Dr.	Cr.
Real cost of goods sold	£10	
Capital re-statement reserve		£10

Thus, under the CPP method, we have the following closing balance sheet:

Closing balance sheet

	£	£		£
Proprietor's capital			Cash	150
Opening balance	100			
Add capital re-statement	10			
	110			
Add profit for the period	40			
		150		
		150		150

Finally, we turn to the *real terms* system. This attempts to combine the two previous methods, by reporting the effect both of specific price changes and of general inflation. The principle behind the double entry is similar, although the practice looks slightly more complicated, because there are two adjustments rather than one:

	Dr.	Cr.
Current cost of goods sold	25	
Real holding gain on stock		15
Capital re-statement reserve		10
	£25	£25

This shows the initial current cost adjustment to cost of sales in the profit and loss account (£25) and the subsequent credit of real holding gains (£15) to arrive at the final profit figure of £40. If required, the credit of the real holding gains would be made to a separate reserve in the balance sheet, rather than to the profit and loss account. The credit to the capital re-statement reserve is made in the balance sheet. Thus, the 'real terms' closing balance sheet is, either the same (in this particular case) as for CPP, or, with real holding gains shown separately, it is:

Closing balance sheet

	£	£		£
Proprietor's capital				
Opening balance	100		Cash	150
Add capital re-statement	10			
	110			
Add real holding gains	15			
	125			
Add operating profit	25			
		150		
		150		150

REVALUATION OF ASSETS

Our illustration hitherto has dealt with a 'cash to cash' example in which there were no non-monetary assets (i.e., those which are not convertible to cash on fixed terms) in the opening balance sheet or in the closing balance sheet. Thus, the net worth of the business was unambiguous in terms of monetary units at the accounting date, and no valuation problem arose. The problem which was analysed was essentially one of *capital maintenance*, i.e., how do we divide the closing net worth (£150 in the example) between that which is necessary to maintain the owner's initial wealth (£110 in terms of the purchasing power of the £ at the start of the period) and the surplus which we describe as profit? We proposed three alternative 'pure' capital maintenance concepts: money capital (£100), current cost of specific capital assets (£125) and general purchasing power (£110). We also considered a fourth approach, 'real terms', which combined the latter two.

These models can also be extended to deal with the valuation of non-monetary assets, whose prices in terms of cash may fluctuate. Such assets are, of course, a usual feature of balance sheets in the practical world of business. In order to illustrate how the valuation problem is dealt with, we shall take our previous example of Old Fred but make the additional assumptions that Fred put an extra £50 into the business at the start of the period, with which he bought a barrow. An appropriate rate of depreciation[7] is 10 per cent per period. Replacement cost at the end of the period (before depreciation) is £60.

On these revised assumptions, the *historical cost* accounts are as follows:

Profit and loss account

	£
Sales	150
Less cost of goods sold	100
Trading profit	50
Less depreciation	5
Net profit	45

Closing balance sheet

	£		£
Proprietor's capital		*Fixed asset*	
Opening balance	150	Barrow, at cost	50
Add profit for the period	45	*Less* accumulated depreciation	5
Closing balance	195		45
		Current asset	
		Cash	150
	195		195

The changes resulting from the revised assumptions are the higher initial capital balance, matched by the cost of the barrow, and the subsequent depreciation of the barrow, which reduces profit (a debit) and increases the depreciation provision against cost, (a credit) in the balance sheet.

The *current cost* (CCA) accounts are as follows:

Current cost profit and loss account

	£
Sales	150
Less current cost of goods sold	125
Current cost trading profit	25
Less current cost depreciation	6
Current cost profit	19

Current cost closing balance sheet

	£		£
Proprietor's capital		*Fixed asset*	
Opening balance	150	Barrow, at current cost	60
Add current cost revaluation		*Less* accumulated	
reserve	35	depreciation	6
	185		54
		Current asset	
Add current cost profit	19	Cash	150
	204		204

There are two differences between current cost and historical cost in this example. The first, which we encountered before, is the adjustment to eliminate stock appreciation, i.e., the difference between the historical cost of goods sold and their current cost at the time of sale. In journal entry form, this adjustment is:

	Dr.	Cr.
Cost of goods sold	£25	
Revaluation reserve		£25

The second difference is the recording of the change in the cost of the barrow between historical cost and current cost. This gives rise to two adjustments. Firstly, the cost of the barrow is re-stated at current cost:

	Dr.	Cr.
Cost of barrow	£10	
Revaluation reserve		£10

Secondly, as a result of this adjustment of cost, the depreciation charge for the current period is adjusted,[8] to reflect current cost rather than historical cost:

	Dr.	Cr.
Depreciation charge	£1	
Accumulated depreciation		£1

The net result of these adjustments is that the balance sheet shows a higher asset valuation than historical cost but a lower balance of profit, the net difference being accounted for by the current cost revaluation reserve.

The *constant purchasing power* (CPP) approach, like the current cost approach (CCA), involves re-stating the fixed asset and the depreciation figure and creating a capital reserve. However, whereas CCA did this on the basis of specific asset prices, CPP does it on the basis of general price level indices. The CPP accounts are as follows:

CPP profit and loss account

	£
Sales	150
Less cost of goods sold	110
Trading profit	40
Less depreciation	5.50
Net profit	34.50

CPP closing balance sheet

	£		£
Proprietor's capital		*Fixed asset*	
Opening balance	150	Barrow, at cost	55
		Less accumulated	
Add CPP re-statement reserve	15	depreciation	5.50
	165		49.50
Add profit for the period	34.50	*Current asset*	
		Cash	150
	199.50		199.50

In the profit and loss account, the historical cost of goods sold is increased by 10 per cent, reflecting general inflation, to £110 in current purchasing power terms. The historical cost depreciation charge is similarly raised by 10 per cent to £5.50. In the balance sheet, initial capital (£150) is supplemented by a 10 per cent reserve (£15) to reflect the maintenance of general purchasing power over the period, and the cost of the barrow is raised by 10 per cent to £55, with accumulated depreciation rising by the same proportion.

The journal entries necessary to translate historical cost into CPP are the same, in debit and credit terms, as those necessary to translate historical cost into CCA, but the index used to calculate amounts is the general index, which rose by 10 per cent over the period, rather than the specific price changes used in the CCA translation. The CPP journal entries are:

	Dr.	Cr.
(1) Cost of goods sold	£10	
CPP re-statement reserve		£10
(2) Cost of barrow	£ 5	
CPP re-statement reserve		£ 5
(3) Depreciation charge	£ 0.50	
Accumulated depreciation		£ 0.50

Thus, the choice between CCA and CPP in a case like this, which involves accounting for non-monetary assets (note that, *during the period*, it is assumed that only stocks and the barrow were owned), depends upon whether we regard specific price adjustment or general price level adjustment as the more appropriate. The former (CCA) tries to capture the current costs of the specific assets used by or held by the business, whereas the latter (CPP) attempts to up-date historical costs in terms of the purchasing power of money. Although CPP has the advantage of relative objectivity, avoiding the problem of assessing the current prices of specific assets, CCA does have the advantage of expressing the values of assets held and used by the business at prices at which they might be expected to change hands currently.

The fourth method of accounting was *real terms* accounting. The accounts on this basis are:

Real terms profit and loss account

		£
Sales		150
Less current cost of goods sold		125
Current cost trading profit		25
Less current cost depreciation		6
Current cost profit		19
Add holding gains:		
Realised holding gain on stocks	25	
Realised holding gain on barrow	1	
Unrealised holding gain on barrow	9	
	35	
Less adjustment for inflation ($£150 \times 0.1$)	15	
Real holding gains		20
Total real gains		39

Real terms closing balance sheet

	£		£
Proprietor's capital		*Fixed asset*	
Opening balance	150	Barrow, at current cost	60
Add capital re-statement reserve	15	*Less* depreciation to date	6
	165		54
		Current asset	
Add total real gains for the period	39	Cash	150
	204		204

The real terms system now yields a different profit figure from the CPP system. The reason for this is that we now have a non-monetary asset (the barrow) in the closing balance sheet. When this is revalued at current cost, an *unrealised holding gain* (£9) is created, and, to the extent that this 'beats the index', it is recorded as a gain (unlike the CCA system, in which any such gain is credited direct to a capital reserve). The extent to which the gain beats the index (and is therefore a real gain) is £4.50 (a money gain of £9, less 10 per cent of original cost, less depreciation, of the asset, £4.50). This is precisely the difference between the 'total real gains' in the real terms system and the net profit in the CPP system.

Thus, relative to the CPP system, the 'real terms' system has the advantage of showing assets at current prices, rather than indexed historical prices. Like CPP, it uses the general index to re-state opening capital on the grounds that the proprietor will wish to judge gain or loss in terms of whether the general purchasing power of his capital has increased or decreased. The difference between non-monetary assets valued at current prices and a capital balance re-stated by means of a general index gives rise to real holding gains and (potentially) losses (as shown in the lower part of the real terms profit and loss account), the unrealised element in these gains (or losses) accounts for the difference between CPP 'net profit' and real terms 'total real gains'.

Relative to CCA, the real terms approach is differentiated by the recognition of *any* holding gains, whether realised or unrealised, as shown in the lower part of the real terms profit and loss account. CCA regards all such gains as being growth of the capital to be maintained, not part of profit, and they are therefore credited direct to the current cost revaluation reserve.

The journal entries necessary to convert historical cost accounts into real terms are as follows. Firstly, we implement the three basic current cost adjustments, but crediting the gains to holding gains, rather than revaluation reserve.

		Dr.	Cr.
(1)	Cost of goods sold	£25	
	Realised holding gain on stocks		£25
(2)	Cost of barrow	£10	
	Realised holding gain on barrow		£ 1
	Unrealised ” ” ” ”		£ 9
		£10	£10
(3)	Depreciation charge	£ 1	
	Accumulated depreciation		£ 1

Finally, we implement the 'real terms', general price level adjustment to opening capital, so that only those holding gains which 'beat inflation' are recognised as gains. The amount of the adjustment is 10 per cent of opening capital:

		Dr.	Cr.
(4)	Capital re-statement reserve (balance sheet)	£15	
	Adjustment for inflation (profit and loss)		£15

We have seen, in this more elaborate example, that our four methods of accounting for charging prices all give different measures of profit or total gain for the period. Historical cost accounting (HCA) which reflects only prices paid in past transactions, shows a net profit of £45. Current cost accounting (CCA), which reflects only current prices and does not recognise any gains which took place in the holding period when the asset was bought and when it was used, shows a net profit of £19, reflecting the higher current cost charges. Constant purchasing power accounting (CPP) up-dates historical cost by means of a general index. Like CCA, it does not show any holding gains on the assets, because they are revalued by the same general index as the capital. Because we have assumed that the general index (used in CPP) rose by less than the specific prices (used in CCA), the increases in costs are less in the CPP case, so that the CPP net profit of £34.50 lies between its HCA (£45) and CCA (£19) counterparts. Finally, the real terms system first calculates CCA profit and then adds in the real holding gains, i.e., the holding gains on assets between purchase (historical cost) and use (current cost), less an adjustment for general inflation. In the present example, this raises Total Real Gains to £39, although in practice there can be holding losses as well as gains, especially when a loss is defined as failure to beat the general price index.

MONETARY ASSETS AND LIABILITIES

The final complication which has been avoided so far is the problem of *monetary* assets and liabilities. We have avoided this by the somewhat unrealistic assumption that Old Fred does not hold money during the period and does not borrow: instead he simply carries a stock of pineapples which are converted to cash (i.e., sold) at the instant before the final balance sheet is drawn up. This was an unrealistic assumption which served the useful purpose of not having to deal with *monetary* assets and liabilities, which might have complicated the exposition too much. However, the time has now come to explore monetary items and, in particular, the 'loss on holding money' and the 'gain on borrowing' which occur in a period of inflation (i.e., decline in the general purchasing power of money).

As a prelude to looking further at monetary items, we shall revert to the algebra used in chapter 2. It will be recalled that the balance sheet identity was:

$$A_t \equiv L_t + N_t$$

and that, over a period of time, the corresponding flow identity was:

$$\Delta_t N \equiv \Delta_t A - \Delta_t L, \text{ or}$$
$$N_t - N_{t-1} \equiv A_t - A_{t-1} - L_t + L_{t-1}$$

where the proprietor did not introduce or withdraw capital, $\Delta_t N$ was identical with profit, i.e.:

$$P_t \equiv A_t - A_{t-1} - L_t + L_{t-1}$$

In the example of Old Fred, as we have so far considered it, there were no liabilities and all of the assets were of a 'non-monetary' type, i.e., they did not have a fixed cash value. In this system, we had the following profit measures:

Historical cost profit:

$$P_{Ht} = A_t - A_{t-1}$$

where A is always measured at historical cost.

Current cost profit:

$$P_{CCt} = A_t.s - A_{t-1}.s$$

where s is the specific price change of each asset held over the relevant period.[9] In our example A_{t-1} was measured at historical cost because the assets were acquired at that time: in a more realistic situation, they would have been acquired earlier and would therefore be measured at current cost at the start of the period (historical cost adjusted by the change of specific price from the time of acquisition to $t-1$).

Constant purchasing power profit:

$$P_{CPPt} = A_t.g - A_{t-1}.g$$

where g is the change in the general purchasing power of money over the relevant period. The qualification given for CCA holds here also: if the assets had not been acquired at $t-1$, then A_{t-1} would have had to have been adjusted by reference to the change in the index (the general index, g, rather than the specific price, s in this case) since original acquisition.

Real terms profit:

$$P_{Rt} = A_t.s - A_{t-1}.g$$

In this case, initial capital, A_{t-1} is adjusted by the general index over the period, whereas closing assets are valued at specific prices. Thus, if the firm simply holds the same assets over the period, there is a real holding gain $(A_{t-1}.(s-g))$ where $s>g$ and a real holding loss $(A_{t-1}.(g-s))$ where $g>s$. Again, strictly A_{t-1} should be expressed in current values at the start of the period.

The next problem is to introduce liabilities, L, and monetary assets M. We shall thus divide assets, A, into monetary, M, and non-monetary, or real, R.

The balance sheet identity is now:

$$R_t + M_t \equiv N_t + L_t$$

and historical cost profit is:

$$P_{Ht} = R_t - R_{t-1} + M_t - M_{t-1} - L_t + L_{t-1}$$

Current cost profit is:

$$Pcc_t = R_t.s - R_{t-1}.s + M_t - M_{t-1} - L_t + L_{t-1}$$

Constant purchasing power profit is:

$$P_{CPPt} = R_t.g - R_{t-1}.g + M_t - M_{t-1}.g - L_t + L_{t-1}.g$$

Real terms profit is:

$$P_{Rt} = R_t.s - R_{t-1}.g + M_t - M_{t-1}.g - L_t + L_{t-1}.g$$

The above four relationships reveal the essence of the alternative approaches to accounting for inflation. They can be summarised in tabular form as follows:

Asset valuation method

		Historical	General index	Specific price
Capital maintenence method	Historical	HC		
	General index		CPP	RT
	Specific price			CCA

This shows how the four models combine different methods of valuation (the amounts at which the assets are shown in the balance sheet) with different methods of capital maintenance (the method of re-stating the opening assets for the purpose of profit calculation). We can see that the first three models fall along the diagonal, indicating that historical cost (HC) makes no adjustment for unrealised price changes either for valuation or capital maintenance purposes, constant purchasing power (CPP) uses general index adjustment of historical costs for both purposes, and CCA uses specific current prices for both purposes. Real terms (RT) is the exceptional case, using specific current prices for asset valuation but a general index for capital maintenance. We could, for completeness, add another hybrid measure to the final column: CCA total gains, which adds total holding gains (rather than real gains, as in the RT model) to CCA income,[10] so that it combines specific price as the valuation method with adjusted opening value as the capital maintenance method. However, this would be untidy in terms of our table because unadjusted opening value is not, in general, the same thing as historical cost (it is current value at the start of the period).

We can use the algebra and the table to draw some conclusions about how monetary items (M and L in our notation) are treated in the different models. Two of the models, HC and CCA involve no special adjustment of monetary items, so that no 'loss on holding money' or 'gain on borrowing' results from inflation. This is because neither of these models makes any adjustment for general inflation. HC makes no adjustment whatsoever for price changes, so that the outcome is not surprising in this case. CCA does make adjustments for specific price changes, but the price of 'monetary' items is, by definition, fixed in terms of money. Hence, the specific prices of these items are constant and they are reported at historical cost, which, because of their constant price, necessarily equals current value.

The remaining two models, CPP and RT do involve special treatment of monetary items, because both involve applying a general index adjustment of all opening capital, whether monetary or non-monetary, for comparison with closing capital, for the purpose of measuring profit or gain. Equally, both involve measuring monetary items in the closing balance sheet at their nominal value, because this is unequivocally both their current value (as in RT) and their historical cost (the basis of CPP). Re-statement of historical values by a general index is not considered an appropriate basis of closing valuations in the CPP case, because such re-statements would be patently wrong: monetary items are, by definition, denominated in *nominal* monetary units (such as £'s), not in real units (i.e., general index adjusted units).

The result of this is that CPP and RT both report a 'gain on borrowing' or 'loss on holding money' in a period of inflation (i.e., a change in the general index). In the case of a monetary asset (such as cash) held throughout a period, the loss on holding money is $M.g$ where M is the nominal amount held and g is the change in the purchasing power of money during the period. In the case of a monetary liability, the gain on borrowing is $L.g$ where L is the nominal amount of the liability.

Thus, only CPP and RT reflect the consequences of pure inflation (g). In order to overcome this apparent deficiency of the CCA system, some of its advocates have tried to adapt it to reflect the gain on borrowing through a 'gearing adjustment' and the loss on holding money through a 'monetary working capital adjustment'. These were features of the 1980 UK standard on current cost accounting (SSAP16) and are discussed in more advanced text books (see chapter 9). It can be argued that they are essentially pragmatic compromises and that the real terms (RT) system is the most logical means of reporting the effects of both specific price changes (as expressed in the valuation of assets) and general inflation (as expressed in the re-statement of opening capital for the purposes of assessing profit or gain).

THE 'GAIN ON BORROWING': A NUMERICAL ILLUSTRATION

In order to make the discussion of 'monetary' items more concrete, we shall illustrate the 'gain on borrowing' by introducing borrowing into the numerical example of Old Fred. It should be remembered that the 'loss on holding money' is the mirror-image of a 'gain on borrowing': i.e., if Fred held an amount of cash which exactly equalled the amount borrowed, the gain on borrowing would be offset exactly by the loss on holding money. This does not mean that it is a sensible policy to hold money and 'hedge' the loss by borrowing in a period of inflation: in practice, an interest rate must be paid on borrowing and this will reflect lenders' expectations of the rate of inflation (the so-called 'Fisher effect'). If lenders anticipate inflation correctly, and, if the 'real' (i.e., inflation-free) rate of interest is positive, then the gain on borrowing will be wiped out by the interest rate, and there will be no surplus left which can be offset against the loss on holding money.

For simplicity, we shall ignore interest by assuming that Fred has received a £50 interest-free loan to buy his cart. A fixed loan also has the advantage of being constant through time, so that the gain on borrowing is correctly estimated by multiplying the initial amount by the appropriate inflation rate (g in our earlier notation).

We have already seen that the *historical cost* out-turn of the business will be unaffected by the loan. We merely attribute £50 of the opening net worth to the long-term loan rather than the proprietor's capital, i.e.:

	Dr.	Cr.
Proprietor's capital	£50	
Long-term loan		£50

The closing balance sheet will record this revised attribution of net worth, but the *change* in the proprietor's interest will be unchanged, an equal amount (£50) being deducted from both the opening and the closing balances.

The same result will obtain for *current cost* (CCA): £50 of net worth will now be attributed to the loan, rather than the proprietor, at both the beginning and the end of the period. In the case of *constant purchasing power* (CPP), we do show a gain on borrowing, as follows:

CPP profit and loss account

	£
Sales	150
Less cost of goods sold	110
Trading profit	40
Less depreciation	5.50
Net profit	34.50
Add gain on borrowing	5.00
CPP net gain	39.50

CPP closing balance sheet

	£		£
Proprietor's capital		*Fixed asset*	
Opening balance	100	Barrow, at cost	55
Add CPP re-statement		*Less* accumulated	
reserve	10	depreciation	5.50
	110		49.50
Add net gain for the period	39.50	*Current asset*	
	149.50	Cash	150.00
Interest-free loan	50.00		
	199.50		199.50

The gain on borrowing appears as an addition (£5) to CPP net profit, to yield what we have euphemistically chosen to describe as 'CPP Net Gain'. Accountants are reluctant to recognise unrealised gains, such as that on borrowing, as 'profit', so 'gain' is a more acceptable term.

The balance sheet reveals the underlying mechanics of the gain on borrowing. We show the proprietor's opening balance as £100 because the assets are now financed partly by a loan of £50. Thus, opening capital is as before £150, but £50 is now loan capital. This becomes important when we apply our inflation adjustments. As before, we adjust the proprietor's opening capital for inflation ($g = 0.1$) but because the capital is lower than in our previous example (£100 rather than £150) so is the amount of the inflation adjustment (£10 rather than £15). The loan financed portion of opening capital (£50) does not require re-statement, because it is fixed in *money* terms. Hence there is a gain on borrowing (£50 × 0.1 = £5) arising from the fact that the loan represents a declining real burden, requiring payment only in devalued currency.

Similar reasoning underlies the *real terms* approach. Here also, an unrealised gain on borrowing appears in the profit and loss account:

Real terms profit and loss account

	£	£
Sales		150
Less current cost of goods sold		125
Current cost trading profit		25
Less current cost depreciation		6
Current cost profit		19
Add holding gains:		
Realised holding gain on stocks	25	
Realised holding gain on barrow	1	
Unrealised holding gain on barrow	9	
	35	
Less adjustment for inflation (£150 × 0.1)	15	
Real gains on non-monetary assets	20	
Add gain on borrowing (£50 × 0.1)	5	
		25
Total real gains		44

Real terms closing balance sheet

	£		£
Proprietor's capital		*Fixed asset*	
Opening balance	100	Barrow, at current cost	60
Add capital re-statement reserve	10	*Less* depreciation to date	6
	110		54
Add total real gains for the period	44	*Current asset*	
	154	Cash	150
Interest-free loan	50		
	204		204

As in the CPP case, the gain on borrowing is added to the 'gains' section of the profit and loss account. It should be noted that the gains on assets still have an adjustment of £15 (=£150 × 0.1) to reduce them to 'real' gains: this is because £150 was the recorded value of those assets at the start of the period. The gain on borrowing arises from the fact that a *liability* did not increase in money amount (remaining constant at £50), whereas it would have had to rise by 10 per cent to be a constant real burden.

The real terms balance sheet, like the CPP balance sheet, shows the proprietor's capital re-stated by 10 per cent but the loan constant in money terms.

AN OVERVIEW

This completes our account of the basic problems and techniques of price change accounting. The broad message to emerge from the analysis of the problems is as follows:

(1) There is a variety of methods of reflecting price changes, and the choice of method is important, because different methods give different results, both for the performance of the business, as represented in the profit and loss account, and the state of the business, as shown in the balance sheet.

(2) It is important to distinguish between the inflation problem and the specific price change problem. The former problem (inflation) is concerned with the decline in the purchasing power of money, the basic unit of measurement. The latter problem (specific price changes) is concerned with the way

specific assets held and used by the firm fluctuate in value, so that, for example, historic cost may not reflect current cost at the time when an asset is used in production or held in the closing balance sheet.

(3) It is also important to distinguish between the capital maintenance concept and the valuation of assets and liabilities. The capital maintenance concept determines the amount of net assets a firm must maintain before a profit is recognised. The valuation concept will determine how the net assets of a firm (i.e., assets less liabilities) are measured at a particular point in time. Thus the measurement of total profit or gain is determined by the interaction between these two concepts.

With regard to the techniques of price change accounting, we saw that the distinction between general inflation and specific price changes could be reflected in a single set of accounts. In particular, it is possible to combine adjustment for specific changes in asset values and for the effect of general price level changes in eroding the purchasing power of opening capital by using a 'real terms' accounting system. Within such a system, it is also possible to incorporate two capital maintenance concepts: a specific price concept which shows operating profit after charging those (specific) current costs necessary to maintain operating capability, and a general price level concept which shows the total gain in the net assets of the business (valued at current prices) expressed in 'real' (constant purchasing power) rather than money terms.

The latter type of system has a great deal to commend it, if we are interested in accounts which represent as closely as possible the underlying economic events and opportunities. However, we did not pay much attention to one problem which underlies systems of current valuation, namely, that current values are often unreliable and expensive to obtain. There is the related problem that alternative measures of current value may differ from one another, i.e., replacement cost, realisable value from sale and value in use (present value of future cash flows obtained from using the assets in the business) may all differ. Much ink has been spilled by accounting theorists (and some by empirical researchers) in assessing the relative merits of alternative valuation methods, and of methods such as 'value to the firm' which combine them. Evaluation of these arguments is outside the scope of this book[11], but the reader should be aware that they draw attention to a possible trade-off between reliability and relevance. Current values may be more relevant for the purposes of many users of accounts, but historical cost may be more reliable. However, our discussions of historical cost methods in earlier chapters should have demonstrated convincingly that the reliability of historical cost is often (as in the case of depreciation) bought at the price of imposing arbitrary rules which reduce its claims to reliability and objectivity. Moreover, in periods of changing prices, current values are likely to be much more relevant than historical cost in assessing the current economic situation of a business. Perhaps, as Keynes is alleged to have said, 'it is better to be approximately right than precisely wrong'.

EXERCISE: PRICE CHANGE ACCOUNTING

A company started operations on 1 January 19x1 with capital of £37,000 made up of three types of asset, each purchased new at that date, as follows:

	£
Plant and machinery	12,000
Stock	20,000
Cash	5,000
	£37,000

Assume the following further information:

(i)   The plant will last for five years, losing value by a constant amount and having no scrap value.
(ii) During the year from 1 January 19x1 to 31 December 19x1 work is carried out on only half of the stock. The wages for this work, amounting to £6,000, are paid on the last day of the year. On the same day, the entire finished stock is sold for £25,000, which is paid in cash, and is replaced by equivalent unprocessed raw material costing £15,000, which is paid for in cash.
(iii) The Retail Price Index was 100 on 1 January and 120 on 31 December 19x1.
(iv) The replacement cost of new plant identical to that owned by the firm rose to £18,000 by 31 December 19x1.

Required

(a)   Prepare a balance sheet and profit and loss account for the year ended 31 December 19x1 on each of the following four bases: historical cost (HC), constant purchasing power (CPP), replacement cost (RC), and real terms

(CPP adjustment of an RC system). Show holding gains as an addition to operating profit, but you need not distinguish realised from unrealised gains.

(b) Comment briefly on the significance of the differences between the various profit figures.

Chapter 8

THE COLLECTION AND PROCESSING OF ACCOUNTING DATA

INTRODUCTION

In earlier chapters, we have concentrated on the end-product of the accounting system: the final accounts which summarise the business firm's activities over a period. In this chapter, we pause briefly to consider how we might ascertain and record the basic facts about the transactions and financial position of a business. Our examples have, hitherto, *assumed* that we have this knowledge, but in practice we will need a carefully designed information system to gather it: otherwise, our accounting records will suffer from avoidable error and, in some cases, fraud. The possibility of error and fraud also exists in the subsequent data processing which takes place within the accounting system. It is therefore desirable that the system contains appropriate cross-checks, and we shall illustrate this with the example of control accounts.

DATA COLLECTION

Information about the basic transactions and events on which the accounting system rests is obtained by a wide range of devices, most of them involving the exchange of paper records. For example, bus passengers are accustomed to receiving tickets in exchange for payment of their fares. The obvious role of the ticket, from the passenger's point of view, is as proof of payment of the fare and, therefore, of the right to travel. Thus one important use of bus tickets is the avoidance of possible fraud by passengers through non-payment of fares. However, the ticket also performs another role, as a receipt for cash received, which serves as the basic record for the bus company's own accounting system. The ticket issuing machine will contain some record of the tickets issued which can be matched against the cash collected as a protection against fraud or error, thus, for example, avoiding the obvious temptation for the bus conductor to keep a share of the fares and under-state the amount collected. The total cash collected, as verified by the tickets issued, will be the amount registered by the accounting system as cash received: this will be debited to cash (an asset in the balance sheet) and credited to receipts (the sales figure in the profit and loss account). The ticket issuing system may, additionally, be a means of gathering *management accounting* data. Modern electronic ticket machines can record detailed information about number, length and time of journeys, which is valuable in assessing the profitability of different services and in planning adjustments to services.

In practice, most business transactions are associated with the issue of a record of some type: to an increasing extent, the record may be of an electronic type, recorded instantaneously in a computer, as, for example, when a bank customer withdraws cash from a bank using an ATM cash dispenser. Traditional paper records include orders, delivery notes, receipts and invoices. All of these can serve the dual purpose of initiating accounting records and of protecting the business against error or fraud. Such records usually enter the accounting system by being listed in what is traditionally called a *book of prime entry*, although the prevalence of computers means that, in practice, this is more likely to be a computer listing than a bound ledger.

DATA PROCESSING

The accounting system processes the data recorded in the books of prime entry, to produce the type of double entry accounts which we examined in earlier chapters. However, the design of the system is not a trivial matter because it is operated by people who may sometimes make errors and occasionally commit fraud. It is therefore important to design the system in such a way that it has as many internal checks as possible, and that there is an appropriate division of labour such that the possibility of undetected fraud is minimised. Computers can be a powerful device for eliminating errors and for introducing automatic checks, but they also bring problems of their own, e.g., the computational power and speed of a computer means that an error in a program can do a great deal of harm in a short time, and a skilled computer fraudster has much more power at his elbow than a fraudulent clerk who has to operate with pen, ink and rubber. Thus, the basic requirement that the accounting system is designed to resist error and fraud remains a central consideration. Another consideration is the information needs of management, e.g., in a business where consumer credit is important, timely data on the amounts of trade debtors outstanding and the age and size of individual debts may be particularly important.

It is not intended here to do more than draw attention to these important issues: specialist texts on accounting systems deal with them in detail. However, it is hoped to give an elementary understanding of how accounting systems work by providing a simple explanation of control accounts, which are one of the oldest devices used by accountants to provide an internal check within the accounting system.

CONTROL ACCOUNTS

A control account is one of the oldest and most basic forms of internal checks. Essentially, it is an aggregate account, prepared from the total of individual entries, and provides a total check on the individual accounts in a ledger. Often there will be a complete system of control accounts, dealing with such items as debtors, creditors, stock and cash. To illustrate how such a system works, we shall use a simple example of a creditors' control account.

Suppose that a company has four suppliers, A, B, C and D, and purchases two types of goods, Y and Z. When the company buys goods this will be recorded by means of various documents, such as written orders (possibly recorded in an order book) and delivery notes (recording the delivery of goods into stock). These will be used for day-to-day management (e.g., in chasing up suppliers who fail to deliver on time) as well as for checking whether the transaction should be recorded in the accounting system. The most important document from an accounting point of view is the *invoice*, which is received from the supplier and (after checking that it is justified by an order and delivery) will be used to initiate the purchase records.

An invoice contains information of the following type:

A. Supply Co. (Supplier)					
To X Manufacturing Co. (Purchaser)					
(Date)	(Units)	(Type)		(Unit price)	(Total)
10 October	4	Y	@	£1	£4

Such invoices will be collected and listed in some way (manually or by computer) to form a *Purchases Day Book*:

Date	Supplier	Units	Type		Amount (£)
10 October	A	4	Y		4
17 "	B	6	Z		12
24 "	C	3	Z		6
31 "	D	8	Y		8
				Total	£30

This provides a complete record of purchases for the period (a month in this example: the number of transactions is unrealistically low, in order to make the example simple). It is what is known, in traditional book-keeping parlance, as a *book of prime entry*, i.e., it is the primary record which initiates the double entry records.

The double entry records are initiated by two separate entries being made (or, in book-keeping language, 'posted') from the book of prime entry. Thus, the main double entry system, or 'nominal ledger' as it is sometimes called, will record the following double entry for the month's transactions:

	Dr.	Cr.
Stock control a/c	£30	
Trade creditors control a/c		£30

In T account form, we have the following:

Stock control a/c

October Purchases   £30 |

Trade creditors control a/c

                    | October Purchases   £30

The two accounts are called 'control accounts' because they represent the total transactions for the month. In order to keep track of individual stocks and creditors for day-to-day management, we shall need more detailed accounts, contained in *personal* or *subordinate ledgers*, to tell us what items are in stock and what amounts are owed to particular suppliers. These records are not part of the main double entry system, but provide a dis-aggregation of the control account data which are part of that system. These accounts are obtained by 'posting' the individual items in the day book, as follows:

Subordinate stock ledger

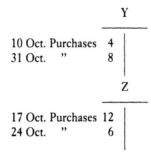

Y

| 10 Oct. Purchases | 4 | |
| 31 Oct. " | 8 | |

Z

| 17 Oct. Purchases | 12 | |
| 24 Oct. " | 6 | |

Subordinate trade creditors ledger[1]

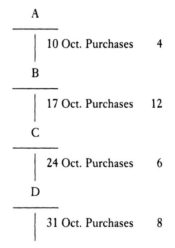

A

| | 10 Oct. Purchases | 4 |

B

| | 17 Oct. Purchases | 12 |

C

| | 24 Oct. Purchases | 6 |

D

| | 31 Oct. Purchases | 8 |

Each item which enters a total appearing on a control account is also recorded in an account in the subordinate ledger. Hence, the balance of a control account should be identically equal to the sum of the balances in the corresponding subordinate ledger. This cross-checking property is an important feature in designing accounting systems. Discrepancies between the control account and the subordinate ledgers will reveal several types of error, e.g., wrong (or absent) postings to individual accounts, or arithmetic errors (e.g., in calculating balances or in summing the book of prime entry). To the extent that different individuals have control over the information which enters the control account and the subordinate ledger, the comparison of the two records can detect certain types of fraud or error. However, the system will not reveal fraud or error which affects both types of accounts, e.g., the entry of a forged invoice (a fraud) or the accidental recording of the same invoice twice in the book of prime entry (an error).

Our example has so far covered only the purchase of stock on credit. Other types of transactions also will be recorded by similar methods, e.g., cash payments to creditors will be listed and posted in aggregate to the trade creditors control account (debit) and to a cash control account (credit). There will also be books of prime entry for goods returned ('returns inwards', which are effectively negative purchases) and discounts received for prompt payment.[2] More advanced text-books give detailed illustrations of such systems. Here we shall confine ourselves to extending the illustration to cover cash payments and discounts received.

Assume that, in the above example, the accounts for suppliers A and B had been settled promptly and discounts have been received. These might be recorded as follows:

Date	Supplier	Discount received	Cash payment
15 October	A	1	3
22 October	B	2	10
		3	13

The cash payments to trade creditors column would be part of the credit side of the cash account. Where a hand-written cash book was kept, the trade creditors' payments would be analysed in a separate column of the cash book, which would be a sub-total of all cash payments. Discounts received are also conveniently recorded in a memorandum column next to the cash payments which gave rise to them, but of course they are not actually part of the cash book because they do not involve the receipt or payment of cash.

The individual items recorded above would be posted to individual trade creditors' accounts in the subordinate ledger, as follows:

Trade creditors ledger

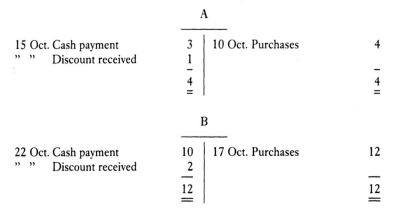

A

15 Oct. Cash payment	3	10 Oct. Purchases	4
" " Discount received	1		
	—		—
	4		4
	=		=

B

22 Oct. Cash payment	10	17 Oct. Purchases	12
" " Discount received	2		
	—		—
	12		12
	=		=

The accounts of C and D are unchanged, with outstanding credit balances of £6 and £8 respectively.

The totals of cash payments and discounts received would be posted to the debit of trade creditors control account[3] as follows:

Trade creditors control account

Oct.	Cash payments	13	Oct. Purchases	30
"	Discounts received	3		
31 Oct. Balances c/d		14		
		—		—
		30		30
		=		=
			1 Nov. Balances b/d	14

The balances are, of course, those owed to C and D (£6 and £8), so that the control account is the sum of the individual accounts.

<h3 style="text-align:center">SUMMARY AND OVERVIEW</h3>

This chapter has drawn the reader's attention to the importance of the system of data collection and processing which is a necessary foundation for accounts. The system is initiated by some form of documentation of the transaction (e.g., an invoice), followed by some form of listing (prime entry) which in turn gives rise to the double entry system ('posting'). The double entry system itself can contain parallel records (personal ledger accounts) which provide detail not available in the aggregate records (control accounts). These parallel records are useful for management and control purposes (e.g., to check on credit management) and the aggregate records provide a cross-check to guard against fraud and error.

The design of accounting information systems is a large subject. Such systems are designed to meet the informational requirements of managers and the users of financial accounts, and at the same time they must contain checks against fraud and error. This should be achieved in a cost-effective manner. Computers have added a new dimension to this subject, by adding to the speed and versatility of data processing and by creating new problems of protecting the information system from access by outsiders. However, the basic principles, described in this chapter in the context of a hand-written accounting system, are still relevant.

One activity which is particularly relevant to the design of the information system is *auditing*. This is concerned with checking the quality and accuracy of financial information. There are two types of auditors, *external* auditors, who are typically employed under the terms of a statute (most often the Companies Act) to check the financial accounts on behalf of shareholders, and *internal* auditors, who are employed by senior management to check on the effectiveness of the firm's information system (and sometimes also on the performance of branches or divisions of a firm). Auditing is always concerned, *inter alia*, with the quality of the information provided and the auditor is therefore concerned with testing the quality of the system which produces the information. It would be far too expensive to check all of the information produced and the auditor will feel more confident that sample checks are adequate if the system producing the information is a good one. Not surprisingly, the emphasis on auditing the system, rather than merely sampling the quality of its output, has increased as computerised accounting systems have become more common.

A list of individual suppliers' balances was prepared from the purchases (i.e. trade creditors) ledger of the Widget Wholesaling Company. These balances were added together, and the total, of £8,506 differed from the balance on the purchase ledger control account at that date.

Further investigation revealed the following errors:

1 A purchases invoice for £52 had not been posted to (i.e., entered in) the supplier's account, although it had been entered in the purchases day book.

2 A purchases invoice for £80 had been entered in the purchases day book twice and posted to the supplier's account twice.

3 A sum of £39 paid to a supplier and correctly entered in the cash book had been posted to his account as £93.

4 There was a casting (i.e., addition) error in the purchases day book, which meant that the total was over-stated by £100.

5 A supplier's account had the credit side overcast by £99.

6 A supplier's balance of £64 had been omitted from the list of balances.

After these errors were corrected, the total of the list of balances agreed with the balance on the control account.

Required

(a) A calculation of the correct amount to be shown in the balance sheet as trade creditors.

(b) A calculation showing how the company's reported profit for the year would be affected by correcting the errors. (Note that the total of the purchases day book would be the purchases figure charged against profit.)

Chapter 9

SOME EXTENSIONS AND SUGGESTIONS FOR FURTHER READING

INTRODUCTION

In this final chapter, we touch upon some important areas which have not been dealt with at all so far and whose proper treatment is beyond the modest aims of this book. We set out to explore what was described as the 'hard core' of the accounting framework. We did not intend to explore the wide range of applications of accounting which exists in the real world, or the wide variety of accounting research. However, this book would be incomplete without the briefest of allusions to other aspects of accounting. In particular, we have not referred to corporate financial reporting, although it is by far the most important area in which financial accountants operate, and we have not discussed the scope of management accounting. The next two sections give the briefest of introductions to these two areas. Finally, there are suggestions for further reading in these areas and the wider field of accounting.

CORPORATE FINANCIAL REPORTING

Most countries have some form of corporate business enterprise which can be created reasonably simply and cheaply by a registration process authorised by statute. In the UK such bodies are known as companies (incorporated under the Companies Acts) and in the USA they are called corporations. The essence of incorporation is that there is a body corporate, which is a legal person separate from the individual members. This enables companies or corporations to own property, make contracts and, in most countries, to have limited liability, i.e., the members (or shareholders) of the limited liability company cannot be made liable, beyond certain limits, for the debts of the company. Moreover, shares in companies can be bought or sold without the company's own assets and liabilities being affected. Thus, companies are a very simple device for bringing together diverse providers of finance in one organisation.

The capital structure of such bodies usually consists of shareholders, who are the ultimate risk-bearers and profit takers, sometimes known as the 'equity' stake, although there may also be preferred ('preference') shares which have more closely defined claims. There are also usually bond or loan stock holders who are legally creditors of the company who contribute interest-bearing loans, which add 'gearing' (in the UK) or 'leverage' (in the USA) to the long-term capital structure.[1] Finally, there are other creditors who are owed money by the company as a result of supplying goods or services. The relationship between these providers of finance and the company is determined by law: the equity shareholders are the ultimate risk-bearers who have the lowest priority of claim on the assets of the company if it is liquidated (i.e., assets sold and debts paid off). To compensate for this, equity shareholders also have the residual claim on any surplus which the company yields, and they are the voting members of the company (sometimes together with preference shareholders) who elect the directors who manage the company. Companies usually have their own constitutions (known in the UK as the Memorandum and Articles of Association) which determine the precise rights, duties and powers of their members and officers. In order to enable the members (i.e., shareholders) of companies to monitor the performance of the directors in managing the company, the directors prepare annual financial statements which are primarily for the use of members, but also for other providers of finance and others (such as employees) with an interest in the firm's affairs. In order to overcome the inevitable 'moral hazard' problem, that directors will be tempted always to paint a picture of successful performance, the accounts are audited by independent auditors. The form and content of accounts and the qualifications of auditors are typically laid down by company law, supplemented in many countries by accounting and auditing standards laid down by independent bodies. In the UK, accounting standards are laid down by the Accounting Standards Board, a private sector body which receives some support from government and some authority from company law (the US equivalent is the Financial Accounting Standards Board), and auditing standards are set by the Audit Practices Committee, an offshoot of a consortium of professional auditing bodies. The International Accounting Standards Committee issues international standards, with the intention of harmonising the efforts of national standard-setting bodies. Another force for international harmonisation is the Commission of the European Community, which has issued a number of directives which will determine the future form of company law, accounting and auditing in member countries.

One important distinction which exists is that between companies whose shares are traded (or 'listed') on a public stock exchange and those whose shares are privately traded. The former type of company typically has the larger shareholder body and also has a greater remoteness of the shareholder from the day-to-day management of the company. In such cases, the shareholders may rely more heavily on the information contained in financial accounts than is the case in smaller, owner-managed firms. Thus, stock exchanges typically impose additional requirements for financial reporting (as in the case of the UK's listing agreement) as a condition of the shares being traded on the exchange.

It is also the case that different countries tend to have different styles of financing and of managing companies, with complementary differences in the law and institutional framework. In the English-speaking countries, for example, there is often a great emphasis on the importance of the ordinary shareholder and (in the case of listed companies) the price of the company's shares on the stock market. In the case of many continental European countries (such as Germany), on the other hand, there is more emphasis on finance by investment bankers, who may hold large blocks of shares or loan stocks, and may be represented by non-executive members of the board of directors. In the latter case, the 'information asymmetry' between directors and providers of finance is much less than in the 'arm's length' stock exchange relationship (as in the UK or the USA) and the importance of the financial reporting process is less. This difference is even reflected in academic research: the USA has been the source of much empirical research in financial accounting, examining the effects of financial reporting on share prices, whereas this type of research has been much less important in Germany and other continental European countries in which financial reporting has been more the province of lawyers and tax specialists.

One peculiar aspect of companies is that they can own or control other companies, known as subsidiary companies. In such a case, the financial statements of the holding company (the centre of ownership and control) will not fully reflect the performance of the group which it controls. Thus, accountants have devised *consolidated accounts* which show the combined performance of the group of companies by, in essence, adding together the components of the accounts of the individual companies in the group and cancelling cross-holdings (such as the holding company's investment in its subsidiaries) and intra-group transactions. Most large companies have subsidiaries, and consolidated accounts are therefore widely used in interpreting the performance of companies listed on the stock exchange. Consolidated accounts involve a number of technical problems (such as the treatment of 'goodwill', which is the excess of the price paid by the holding company for a subsidiary's shares over the 'book' value, i.e., net worth recorded in the balance sheet). Some of these problems have recently given rise to various 'creative accounting' devices, and the whole area of group accounting is currently one of controversy and change.

FINANCIAL ACCOUNTING THEORY

The earlier chapters of this book concentrated on the internal logic of the financial accounting framework. Sometimes, notably in chapter 6 on interpretation of accounts and chapter 7 on accounting for price changes, it was necessary to refer to relevance to the needs of users of accounts, but these needs were not specified with much precision and the nature of the relevance of accounting data was not explored in any depth. Such questions are the province of financial accounting theory, and a proper discussion of them is outside the scope of this book, although the present author has addressed them elsewhere.[2] However, we shall consider the briefest of outlines, to give some idea of the flavour of the subject.

Financial accounting theory has developed in three broad forms, each of which we shall describe in turn. These are: firstly, empirical inductive theory, which tries to derive general principles from observation of existing practices; secondly, deductive theory, which makes assumptions about user needs and deduces forms of accounting data which will meet those needs; thirdly, the new empiricism, which attempts to assess the usefulness of accounting data by examining their impact on share prices.

The empirical inductive method is the oldest form of accounting. It was natural for accountants and writers on accounting to indulge in *ex post* rationalisation of actual practice, partly as a means of self-justification and partly as a means of explaining practice. Thus, such concepts as accrual accounting, realisation, matching and prudence, all of which have been touched upon in earlier chapters, were derived from observation of actual practice, rather than being the original motivation behind practice. However, there is an important feedback from such theory to practice: once a concept has been derived from current practice, it can be used as a guiding principle in evaluating new practices or changes in existing practices. For this reason, the empirical inductive approach still plays an important part in the development of accounting practice, particularly in the deliberations of professional bodies, standards committees and others who are concerned to standardise accounting by defining what is considered to be good practice.

A later development in financial accounting theory was the deductive method. This was associated with a desire to define which accounting method would best meet users' needs, and it also tended to draw heavily on the ideas and methods of economic theorists. Thus, there has been much debate on the appropriate definitions of such central concepts as income, cost and value, e.g., there has been an extensive exploration of the relationship between the accounting rate of return and the economic rate of return. Much of this was associated with the problem of accounting for price changes. The debate on these issues continues, but it has become apparent that there are no simple 'correct' solutions. In a world characterised by heterogeneous users of accounts and by imperfect and incomplete markets, we are unlikely to be able to discover single-value summary measures of income or value which will meet all users' needs at all times. Thus, the high hopes of some early writers on the subject have not been fulfilled, although a much better insight has been obtained into the properties of different types of accounting information. More recently, the deductive approach to accounting theory has been enriched by new ideas from economics, notably the economics of information and agency theory, which have offered a deeper understanding of the role of accounting information and the case for (and against) regulating its supply.

The most recent development, the new empiricism has dominated academic research in the subject, particularly in North America, in recent years. This has taken many forms, but the most common is to assess the impact of a particular piece of accounting information on share price returns, using some form of market model (derived from finance theory) to calculate an 'other things being equal' measure of expected returns. The models used for these empirical tests are based on some quite subtle assumptions, and the empirical data are never ideal (since controlled experiments are not possible), so that it is not surprising that the interpretation of the results is controversial. Thus, the results of the new empiricism, like those of deductive theory, have not yet fulfilled the high hopes of some of its earlier protagonists who hoped that empirical research would resolve or avoid the intellectual squabbles of the deductive theorists. Nevertheless, much has been learned from empirical research. It is, for example, comforting to know that accounting information *does* appear to be reflected in share prices.

In summary, accounting theory is still in its infancy, but it is making progress. It has gone substantially through the initial stages of naive optimism, comparable with that of early natural scientists who hoped to find the philosopher's stone[3] or the elixir of life. It is now in a more mature stage, in which we are, at least, becoming aware of what we do *not* know.

MANAGEMENT ACCOUNTING

Management accounting is prepared by management for the use of management. It is therefore relatively free of the 'moral hazard' problems which arise in financial reporting and it is virtually untouched and unconstrained by law or regulation. It is also heterogeneous in form, reflecting the activities and organisational features of the individual firm to which it relates (an idea made specific by the recent development of a 'contingency theory' of management accounting). Finally, because its concern is to inform the present actions of management, which will have consequences in the future, it tends to be more forward-looking in its orientation than financial accounting, which has typically concentrated on *ex post* reporting of transactions. However, management accounting is also concerned with monitoring the consequences of decisions and therefore deals in data relating to the past and the present, as well as the future.

One of the oldest areas of management accounting is cost accounting, which deals with identifying the cost of productive processes, for the purposes both of controlling costs and of assisting pricing and output decisions. For control purposes, cost accountants have devised elaborate standard costing schemes which identify the sources of variation of the actual costs of production from the target (or standard) level. The identification of relevant costs for the purposes of pricing and output decisions has been the subject of much attention and debate. In some circumstances, it may be profitable to take on work at a price which covers marginal (i.e. incremental) cost but not average cost, although, in the long run, the survival of the business depends upon its recovering enough revenue to cover all costs, including those which are fixed (i.e., not incremental) in the short term. There has also been much debate on the allocation of joint costs (such as a shared production facility) and joint revenues between processes or activities which are being appraised independently (as in the exercise at the end of chapter 6). Finally, there are a variety of techniques available for the identification and measurement of costs, including statistical estimation methods.

Another important area of management accounting is budgeting, i.e., estimating future financial flows. This can be done either for decision-making purposes, to demonstrate the probable future consequences of decisions, or for control purposes, comparing the actual outcome with the budget in order to assess the extent to which past decisions are being carried out successfully. The most fundamental form of budget is a cash budget, which estimates future cash flows and therefore gives a view of the firm's liquidity and solvency over a future period. The term 'budgeting' is also used in the context of investment appraisal, which is commonly known as 'capital budgeting'. This is because investment involves the outlay of cash (or foregoing the opportunity to receive cash) in exchange for future receipts of cash (or saving of cash expenditure). Thus, an appraisal of whether the investment is worthwhile depends upon estimating future returns, which is a budgetary process.

The methods and theory of management accounting have changed greatly over recent years, although it is possible that academics, who are responsible for developing new methods and theories, over-estimate the extent to which new ideas percolate into practice. Traditional methods are based upon elaborate book-keeping techniques and typically involve the detailed allocation of full costs, as in standard costing systems. These methods were challenged from the nineteen-twenties onwards by ideas derived from economic theory, which sought to identify those costs which were relevant to particular purposes. Thus, concepts such as marginal cost, avoidable cost and opportunity cost crept into the literature (and, more slowly, into practice), supplementing the traditional belief that an elaborate enough system could identify 'true cost', and replacing it with the more flexible principle of 'different costs for different purposes'. The economist's approach also offered insights into the measurement of divisional performance in large, divisionalised companies, where it might be considered important to have divisional performance measures and targets which are consistent with those appropriate for the firm as a whole.

Another source of new approaches to management accounting,

which has been important in the period since the Second World War is operational research, the broad collection of mathematical and statistical techniques concerned with maximising operational efficiency. A notable example of operational research techniques which have a place in management accounting is mathematical programming. Many simple resource allocation problems can, for example, be characterised as linear programming problems. Linear programming provides optimal solutions to such problems, thus avoiding the need for an internal price system, but there is a large literature on how 'shadow prices' derived from linear programming[4] can be used for internal resource allocation decisions, where continuous resort to an optimisation programme is infeasible. Another example of an operational research model is the optimal inventory control model, which attempts to calculate the optimal stock-holding level, given the level and degree of uncertainty of demand, the lag in supply, and the costs of holding stock (e.g., interest on capital tied up) and of running out of stock (lost sales). Statistical methods of estimating cost relationships (e.g., by regression analysis of the relationship between output and various components of cost), which have already been referred to, can also be classified broadly as operational research techniques.

Following the impact of economics and then of operational research, described in the previous two paragraphs, there has been a third wave of new ideas and approaches to management accounting. This could be characterised as being associated with a sociological perspective on management accounting. It views management accounting as a human activity arising out of and influencing human relationships within the context of an organisation, or the wider context of society. It is sometimes characterised as a 'behavioural' approach to accounting, and it affords some important insights into management accounting.

A mundane example which is nevertheless of considerable practical importance is the impact of budgeting within an organisation. The traditional attitude of the accountant to budgets was authoritarian: once a budget was set it should be complied with, and typically that meant that it would impose an upper limit on expenditure. The budget was therefore (in addition to its role in planning and decision-making) a device for controlling expenditure, and, in particular, reducing it below the level to which it might rise in the absence of the budget constraint. However, in practice, even casual observation suggests that the budgetary process can actually increase expenditure. The accountant setting the budget may regard the budgetary target as a maximum but the person who is given the budget may regard it as a minimum, if the system offers no rewards for saving on the budget level. There are at least two possible reasons for this: firstly, the rewards of a high level of expenditure (a more comfortable working environment), and secondly the possible 'knock-on' effect of not spending the full budget, if the next period's target is based on the previous period's expenditure. This suggests that the budgetary process should be approached in a thoughtful manner which takes account of organisational structure and human relations, rather than as a mechanical process of minimising the cost of a given output in a system with known fixed parameters.

A whole range of approaches has been developed for analysing the human and organisational factors in management accounting. One of these is the agency theory approach, derived from neoclassical economic theory, which considers the design of reward structures which will bring the aims of the agent (the person managing the budget in our example) into line with those of the principal (top management, which sets the budget). Other approaches rely more on sociological, political or historical analysis and include contingency theory (relating the form of the management accounting system to the characteristics of the particular organisation), historical critiques (such as the notable work of Professors Kaplan and Johnson,[5] which shows how management accounting practices have evolved from historical needs and may therefore tend to lag behind new needs), and 'critical theories' which tend to regard accounting as an expression of and vehicle for power relationships between different groups in society. This rich variety of ideas takes us very far from the popular image of the dull, conventional accountant whose sole concern is with the numerical accuracy of historical records of transactions.

SOME SUGGESTIONS FOR FURTHER READING

In this final section of the book, there are suggestions for further reading, both to reinforce the basic techniques covered in the book and to introduce the reader to more advanced and wider aspects of accounting.

The basic techniques of accounting have been introduced in this book using essentially the same approach as that adopted by Prof. H. C. Edey in his *Introduction to Accounting* (Hutchinson, 4th edition, 1978).[6] This can be recommended particularly for more detailed treatment of some issues and a good set of worked examples and exercises. A more lengthy and comprehensive first-year text-book on financial accounting is John Arnold, Tony Hope and Alan Southworth, *Financial Accounting* (Prentice Hall, 1985) and its sister text-book, Arnold and Hope's *Accounting for Management Decisions* (Prentice Hall, 2nd edition, 1990) can be recommended as an introductory management accounting text. Another introductory management accounting text, with a greater organisational and behavioural emphasis, is David Otley, *Accounting Control and Organisational Behaviour* (Heinemann, 1987).

More advanced expositions of accounting systems and financial accounting are provided in many text-books. One book which can be particularly recommended is A. D. Barton, *The Anatomy of Accounting* (3rd edition, University of Queensland Press, 1984).

In the area of company accounting, two excellent introductions to UK company accounts and their interpretation are R. H. Parker's *Understanding Company Financial Statements* (3rd edition, Penguin, 1988) and P. Bird and B. Rutherford's *Understanding Company Accounts* (3rd edition, Pitman, 1989). Both of these books reproduce and interpret real examples of company accounts, although readers must bear in mind that UK companies represent only one example of a variety of international practice. An advanced text on the interpretation of financial accounts which is American in origin but travels well internationally is George Foster, *Financial Statement Analysis* (2nd edition, Prentice Hall, 1986). This book also introduces some more advanced technical ideas and the results of empirical research in the area of financial reporting.

More advanced treatments of price change accounting, including discussion of theoretical issues which were avoided in chapter 7, will be found in W. T. Baxter's *Inflation Accounting* (Philip Allan, 1984) and in a book by the present author, G. Whittington, *Inflation Accounting, An Introduction to the Debate* (Cambridge University Press, 1983). An introductory survey of wider aspects of accounting theory is provided by the present author's paper in *The British Accounting Review*, Autumn 1986.

The regulation and reform of financial accounting has recently been a topic of considerable interest in most advanced market economies. Some of the current problems of financial accounting in the UK are described and illustrated in a very readable manner in Ian Griffiths' best-selling book *Creative Accounting, or how to make your profits what you want them to be* (Sidgwick and Jackson, 1986). Proposals for the reform of financial reporting practice will be found in the Solomons Report (David Solomons, *Guidelines for Financial Reporting*, the Institute of Chartered Accountants in England and Wales, 1989) and a report by the Research Committee of the Institute of Chartered Accountants of Scotland, *Making Corporate Reports Valuable* (Kogan Page, 1988).

Accounting is a very varied activity which has been the subject of a great deal of research and development in recent years. There are whole areas of application (such as public sector accounting, with its recent emphasis on 'value for money' auditing) which have not even been mentioned in this book. The flavour of some of these areas and an indication of the form and direction of some current research is presented in a form which is both palatable and digestible in Bryan Carsberg and Tony Hope (editors), *Current Issues in Accounting* (2nd edition, Philip Allan, 1984), and in a companion book edited by David Ashton, Trevor Hopper and Robert Scapens, *Topics in Management Accounting* (Prentice Hall, 1991). The references in these books provide suggestions for further reading.

Finally, the reader who is interested in the accounting profession and even possibly in a career as an accountant will find guidance in Christopher Nobes' *Becoming an Accountant* (Longman, 1983) and *Accounting Explained* (with John Kellas, Penguin, 1990). These books are written in the context of the UK, and the accounting profession, like company law, is an institution whose details vary across countries. However, the underlying principles and functions are usually the same, and the accounting profession has followed the example of companies in straddling many national boundaries.

SOLUTIONS TO EXERCISES

(1)   *The balance sheet*

**Adam Ferguson
Balance sheet
as at 31 October**

	£	£		£	£
Capital			*Fixed assets*		
Proprietor's capital		1,400	Motor vehicle		1,000
Long-term loans			*Current assets*		
David Hume	1,200		Stock in trade	950	
Bank	300		Trade debtors	600	
			Cash in hand	800	
		1,500			
Current liabilities					2,350
Trade creditors		450			
		£3,350			£3,350

147

(2)
Horizontal format

William Robertson
Balance sheet
as at 31 October

	£	£		£	£
Capital account			*Fixed assets*		
Proprietor's capital		1,000	Freehold buildings		1,400
Long-term loan		600	*Current assets*		
			Stock in trade	900	
Current liabilities			Trade debtors	1,900	
Trade creditors	1,500		Cash in hand	100	
Bank overdraft	1,200				
		2,700			2,900
		£4,300			£4,300

Vertical format

William Robertson
Balance sheet
as at 31 October

	£	£	£
NET ASSETS EMPLOYED			
Fixed assets			
Freehold buildings			1,400
Current assets			
Stock in trade	900		
Trade debtors	1,900		
Cash in hand	100		
		2,900	
Less current liabilities			
Trade creditors	1,500		
Bank overdraft	1,200		
		2,700	
Net current assets			200
			£1,600

FINANCED BY:
Capital account
  Proprietor's capital   1,000
Long-term loan   600

£1,600

(3) Balance sheet after the six transactions

	£	£	£
NET ASSETS EMPLOYED			
Fixed assets			
Freehold buildings		1,400	
Office equipment		300	
			1,700
Current assets			
Stock in trade	300		
Trade debtors	1,000		
Cash in bank	350		
Cash in hand	100		
		1,750	
Less current liabilities			
Trade creditors		1,050	
Net current assets			700
			£2,400
FINANCED BY:			
Capital account			
Proprietor's capital		1,000	
Plus profit for period		600	
		1,600	
Less drawings		200	
			1,400
Long-term loans			1,000
			£2,400

(4)

William Robertson
Flow of funds statement
for November

	£
Sources	
Profit	600
Additional long-term loans	400
Reduction of stock	600
Received from debtors	900
	£2,500

	£
Uses	
Proprietor's drawings	200
Purchase of office equipment	300
Net payments to trade creditors	450
Increase in cash in bank	1,550
	£2,500

3 THE ACCOUNTING SYSTEM: ELEMENTS OF DOUBLE ENTRY ACCOUNTING

David Hume

Double entry

Transaction	Bank		Debtors		Stock		Creditors		Profit and loss		Proprietor	
	Dr.	Cr.	Dr.	Cr.	Dr.	Cr.	Dr.	Cr.	Dr.	Cr.	Dr.	Cr.
1	1,000											1,000
2		150			150							
3		20							20			
4			80			50				30		
5	40					50			10			
6					120			120				
7		15									15	
8	40			40								
9	35		35			50				20		
10			50			30				20		
Total	1,115	185	165	40	270	180		120	30	70	15	1,000
Balance	930		125		90			120		40		985

Trial balance after transaction 10

	Dr.	Cr.
Bank	930	
Debtors	125	
Stock	90	
Creditors		120
Profit and loss		40
Proprietor		985
	£1,145	£1,145

Balance Sheet
after transaction 10

Current assets	£	£
Bank	930	
Trade debtors	125	
Stocks	90	
		1,145
Less current liabilities		
Trade creditors		120
Net current assets		1,025
Financed by:		
Proprietor's interest		
Capital account	985	
Profit for the period	40	
		1,025

The profit for the period, according to the balance on the profit and loss account, is £40.

This is made up as follows:

Trading profits (less loss)	£60
Less rent	20
Net profit	£40

There are various assumptions behind this calculation. Each arises out of the valuation of an item in the Balance Sheet. The obvious assumptions are:

1 That the valuation of stocks at historic cost is appropriate. Resale value of stocks may be higher or lower than this amount, and replacement cost also may be different from historic cost. Either of these alternative methods of valuation might be considered appropriate in certain circumstances.

2 That the rent of £20 was in respect of the precise period ending at transaction 10. If it covered a longer period, the balance sheet should show an appropriate payment in advance as an asset, and a corresponding deduction should be made from the amount of rent charged to the profit and loss account. If it covered a shorter period, an accrued liability for rent should appear in the balance sheet, and the rent charged to profit and loss should be correspondingly higher.

Another assumption, which again arises out of the valuation of an asset, is the possibility of bad debts. If Robertson or Ferguson is unable to pay his debt, the item 'Trade debtors' is over-stated, and a provision for bad debts should be deducted from this asset, a corresponding charge being made to the Profit and Loss Account.

4 THE ACCOUNTING SYSTEM: REVENUES AND EXPENSES

Grantchester Gaskets

Trial balance as at 1 January 19__

	Dr. £	Cr. £
Stocks		
Raw materials	350	
Work-in-progress	250	
Finished goods	300	
Trade debtors	500	
Trade creditors		320
Cash at bank	390	
Equipment	800	
Proprietor's capital		2,270
	£2,590	£2,590

		£			£
		Raw Materials			
1 Jan.	Balance b/d	350	31 Jan.	Work in progress	20
6 "	Trade creditors	90	31 "	Balance c/d	420
		440			440
	Balance b/d	420			

		£			£
		Work in Progress			
1 Jan.	Balance b/d	250	16 Jan.	Finished goods	120
7 "	Cash	20	31 "	Balance c/d	240
14 "	Cash	20			
21 "	Cash	20			
28 "	Cash	20			
31 "	Cash	10			
31 "	Raw materials	20			
		360			360
	Balance b/d	240			

		Finished goods			
1 Jan.	Balance b/d	300	3 Jan.	Cost of sales	80
16 "	Work-in-progress	120	24 "	Cost of sales	200
			31 "	Balance c/d	140
		420			420
	Balance b/d	140			

		Cost of sales			
3 Jan.	Finished goods	80	31 Jan.	Trading account	280
24 "	Finished goods	200			
		280			280

		Trade debtors			
1 Jan.	Balance b/d	500	11 Jan.	Cash	200
3 "	Sales	100			
24 "	Sales	280	31 "	Balance c/d	680
		880			880
	Balance b/d	680			

		Sales			
31 Jan.	Trading account	380	3 Jan.	Trade debtors	100
			24 "	Trade debtors	280
		380			380

		Equipment			
1 Jan.	Balance b/d	800			

£   £

Cash

		£			£
1 Jan.	Balance b/d	390	7 Jan.	Wages and work-in-progress	40
11 "	Trade debtors	200	14 "	Wages and work-in-progress	40
			21 "	Wages and work-in-progress	40
			23 "	Trade creditors	120
			28 "	Wages and work-in-progress	40
			31 "	Rent and work-in-progress	20
			31 "	Balance c/d	290
		590			590
	Balance b/d	290			

Trade creditors

23 Jan.	Cash	120	1 Jan.	Balance b/d	320
31 "	Balance c/d	290	6 "	Raw materials	90
		410			410
				Balance b/d	290

Wages

7 Jan.	Cash	20	31 Jan.	Profit and loss	80
14 "	Cash	20			
21 "	Cash	20			
28 "	Cash	20			
		80			80

Rent

31 Jan.	Cash	10	31 Jan.	Profit and loss	10

Trading account

31 Jan.	Cost of sales	280	31 Jan.	Sales	380
31 "	Profit and loss	100			
		380			380

	£		£
	Profit and loss		
31 Jan. Wages	80	31 Jan. Trading account	100
31 " Rent	10		
31 " Proprietor's capital	10		
	100		100

	Proprietor's capital		
31 Jan. Balance c/d	2,280	1 Jan. Balance b/d	2,270
		31 " Profit and loss	10
	2,280		2,280
		Balance b/d	2,280

Trading and
Profit and loss account
for January 19__

		£	£
Sales			380
Less: Cost of sales			280
Gross profit			100
Less: Expenses			
Wages		80	
Rent		10	
			90
Net profit			10

Balance sheet
as at 31 January

	£	£
Fixed assets		
Equipment (at cost)		800
Current assets		
Stocks and work-in-progress	800	
Trade debtors	680	
Cash	290	
	1,770	
Less current liabilities		
Trade creditors	290	
Net current assets		1,480
Net assets		2,280
Financed by:		
Proprietor's capital		2,270
Add profit for the month		10
		2,280

---

5 THE ACCOUNTING SYSTEM: ACCRUALS, PREPAYMENTS
AND DEPRECIATION *GEORGE SQUARE*

Outline solution

Journal entries (ledger accounts can be derived from these, and are not given here)

Transaction	Account	Dr. £	Cr. £
1	Office premises	4,000	
	Long-term mortgage loan		4,000
2	Raw materials	3,000	
	Bank		2,200
	Trade creditors		800
3	Wages	4,000	
	Bank		4,000
	Work-in-progress	2,500	
	Wages		2,500

Transaction	Account	£ Dr.	£ Cr.
4	Work-in-progress	2,700	
	Raw materials		2,700
5	Finished goods	3,000	
	Work-in-progress		3,000
6	Factory rent	300	
	Bank		300
	Work-in-progress	300	
	Factory rent		300
7	Drawings	400	
	Bank		400
8	Insurance	600	
	Bank		600
	Work-in-progress	200	
	Insurance		200
9	Electricity	900	
	Bank		900
	Electricity	100	
	Accrued charges		100
	Work-in-progress	750	
	Electricity		750
10	Cost of sales	2,500	
	Finished goods		2,500
	Trade debtors	6,000	
	Sales		6,000
	Bank	7,000	
	Trade debtors		7,000
11	Depreciation expenses (machinery)	250	
	Accumulated depreciation (machinery)		250
	Depreciation expenses (office)	500	
	Accumulated depreciation (office)		500
12	Interest	400	
	Bank		400

No trial balance is given here, but the ledger balances all appear in the accounts, and the fact that they balance proves that the trial balance would have balanced.

George Square
Trading and profit and loss account
for the year ended 31 December

	£		£
Cost of sales	2,500	Sales	6,000
Gross profit	3,500		
	6,000		6,000
Depreciation	750	Gross profit	3,500
Insurance	400		
Electricity	250		
Wages	1,500		
Interest	400		
	3,300		
Net profit	200		
	3,500		3,500

George Square
Balance sheet
as at 31 December

	Cost £	Aggregate depreciation £	£	(1 Jan ...) £
Fixed assets				
Office premises	4,000	500	3,500	
Machinery	2,500	750	1,750	(2,000)
	6,500	1,250	5,250	
Current assets				
Stock-raw materials	1,500			(1,200)
Work-in-progress	4,850			(1,400)
Stock-finished goods	1,200			(700)
Trade debtors	500			(1,500)
		8,050		
Less Current liabilities				
Trade creditors	3,100			(2,300)
Sundry creditors	100			
Bank overdraft	3,050			(1,250)
		6,250		
Net current assets			1,800	
Net assets			7,050	(3,250)
Financed by:				
Proprietor's capital				
Balance at January			3,250	
Plus profit for year			200	
			3,450	
Less drawings			400	
			3,050	(3,250)
Long-term mortgate loan			4,000	–
			7,050	(3,250)

Flow of Funds Statement
for the year ended 31 December

(1) *Format emphasising cash*

	£	£	£
Sources			
Profit	200		
Plus depreciation	750		
Net funds from operations		950	
Long-term mortgage loan		4,000	
Net payments received from debtors		1,000	
Increase in credit received		900	
			6,850
Less uses			
Purchase of office premises		4,000	
Increase in stocks: raw materials	300		
Work-in-progress	3,450		
Finished goods	500		
		4,250	
Drawings		400	
			8,650
Increase in bank overdraft			1,800

(2)   *Alternative format, emphasising change in working capital*

Sources	£	£	£
Profit	200		
Plus depreciation	750		
Net funds from operations		950	
Long-term mortgage loan		4,000	
			4,950
Less uses			
Purchase of office premises		4,000	
Proprietor's drawings		400	
			4,400
			550
Net increase in working capital			
Increase in stocks: Raw materials	300		
Work-in-progress	3,450		
Finished goods	500		
		4,250	
Less Net payments received from debtors	1,000		
Increase in credit received	900		
Increase in bank overdraft	1,800		
		3,700	
			550

The assessment of performance appears below, under chapter 6.

6 THE INTERPRETATION OF ACCOUNTS

(1)   *George Square*
     Assessment of performance

It is important to remember two principles when interpreting financial statements:

   (1)   The information should be looked at as a whole, i.e., individual ratios cannot be interpreted in isolation from one another, and neither can the different financial statements.
   (2)   The financial statements themselves are only part of the information which we would use to assess performance, so that our interpretation will be contingent on unknown factors, such as the type of business this

firm is involved in, the past record of the firm, current plans and future prospects.

Looking at the financial statements gives us the following initial facts:

Profit and loss account

Sales seem rather low in relation to assets employed and the profit margin is handsome (3,500/6,000). However, we would like to know the nature of the business before making a final judgement. The net profit margin is much lower and so is the rate of return on assets employed, partly because of depreciation and interest charge on the new office premises. This could mean that there is scope for increasing sales without much increase in overheads (i.e., the firm may not be at the lowest cost point of its short-run average cost curve), e.g., an optimistic suggestion would be that sales could double without overheads increasing, in which case gross profit would rise to £7,000, and net profit to £3,700 (more than twelve times the present level).

Balance sheet

This shows an illiquid closing position, insofar as there is a substantial bank overdraft, but, on the other hand, current assets exceed current liabilities. The reason for this is the high level of stocks and work-in-progress. Crucial questions here are how quickly and cheaply the work-in-progress can be converted to finished goods, and how marketable will those finished goods be? If the answers are favourable, the firm is in a strong position; if not, it is decidedly vulnerable. The long-term capital also contains a high level of gearing (4,000/7,050), and the security of the creditors, if things do turn out badly, may well depend upon the market value (as opposed to the balance sheet value) of the fixed assets.

The flow of funds statement

This adds a dynamic element to the static position portrayed by the balance sheet. Both formats show modest net funds generated by operations (£950, including £750 from the adding back of depreciation) which are more than absorbed by the increase in stocks and work-in-progress. The big increase in the latter item emphasises the crucial importance of the firm being able to make future sales at a profitable price. The purchase of premises is a large use of funds which can be expected not to recur, but this was financed by the loan which is also unlikely to be repeated, given the firm's high gearing ratio and the consequent limited liability to cover interest payments. The increase in the bank overdraft is large for a firm of this size (and would, in practice, give rise to high interest charges which have not been specified here), so that the overall flow of funds picture is one of an unhealthy drift towards illiquidity.

Summary

There are signs of potential profitability (in the gross profit margin) and the increased output which will be necessary to realise it (the increase in work-in-progress). However, current net profits are poor and the firm is in a dangerously illiquid position. Everything depends upon future sales, prices and costs. This firm is a decidedly risky proposition.

(2) *The Tennis Court*

Double entry system

Transaction	Bank Dr.	Bank Cr.	Proprietor Dr.	Proprietor Cr.	Land and buildings Dr.	Land and buildings Cr.	Bar equipment Dr.	Bar equipment Cr.	Profit and loss Dr.	Profit and loss Cr.	Stock wines Dr.	Stock wines Cr.	Creditors Dr.	Creditors Cr.
1				3000	3000									
2				500	500									
3							1000							1000
4	2000									2000				
5	1850	500								1850				
6									400		500			
7		1250							1250			400		
8		250							250					
9		300	300											
10		300							500					
11		450							450					200
12	1600									1600				
Total	5450	3050	300	3500	3500	–	1000	–	2850	5450	500	400	–	1200
Balance	2400			3200	3500		1000			2600	100			1200

Trial balance after transaction 12

	Dr.	Cr.
Bank	2,400	
Proprietor		3,200
Land and buildings	3,500	
Bar equipment	1,000	
Profit and loss		2,600
Stock (Wines)	100	
Creditors		1,200
	£7,000	£7,000

Balance sheet after transaction 12

	£	£
Fixed assets		
Land and buildings	3,500	
Bar equipment	1,000	
		4,500
Current assets		
Stock	100	
Bank	2,400	
	2,500	
Less current liabilities		
Trade creditors	1,200	
NET CURRENT ASSETS		1,300
NET ASSETS		5,800
Financed by:		
Proprietor's interest		
Proprietor's account	3,500	
Plus profit for year	2,600	
	6,100	
Less drawings	300	
		5,800

Profit and loss account

	£		£
Cost of wines sold	400	Gross revenue	5,450
Cost of food sold	500		
Groundsman's wages	1,250		
Barman's wages	250		
Catering wages	450		
	2,850		
Net profit	2,600		
	5,450		5,450

Detailed profit and loss account

	£	£
Tennis court		
Fee income	2,000	
Less groundsman's wages	1,250	
Net profit		750
Bar		
Sales of wines and spirits	1,850	
Less cost of wine and spirits	400	
	1,450	
Less bar wages	250	
NET PROFIT		1,200
Restaurant		
Restaurant takings	1,600	
Less cost of food sold	500	
	1,100	
Less catering wages	450	
NET PROFIT		650
TOTAL NET PROFIT		2,600

Points for discussion

1 Should the bar equipment be charged against bar profits? If so, how should we decide on the appropriate depreciation rate?
2 Is all the stock saleable? If some deterioration has occurred, by how much should the value of stock be reduced?

3 Should the repair of the pavilion be considered to be part of the purchase price (i.e., a low price for a building in poor condition) or should it be considered part of the annual expense of running a club, i.e., necessary annual maintenance?

4 Does the proprietor spend time running the club which is not charged as a cost, although it represents a sacrifice of earnings in alternative employment?

5 Should any part of the cost of the pavilion be charged to the tennis court, restaurant or bar? If so, how should this cost be apportioned?

6 How can the most profitable section of the business be determined, e.g., should all of the subscriptions be considered to be the fee income of the tennis court or should some be considered to relate to the bar or restaurant? Is 'money' profit the acid test of which section is the most profitable?

Note that the above discussion points take the form of questions rather than answers. The answers will depend partly on fact (e.g., what is the state of the stock?), partly on judgement (e.g., what is the appropriate depreciation pattern for bar fittings?) and partly on a more precise definition of the purpose for which the information is to be used (e.g., if we are considering terminating a particular activity, we should take account of all the *additional* costs and benefits to the business flowing from the activity. This means, for example, that we should take account of the fact that each activity probably attracts business for the others and, on the other hand, some fixed costs may not be avoidable even if an activity is terminated).

7 ACCOUNTING FOR PRICE CHANGES

Price change accounting exercise

(i)   *Profit and loss account*

	(1) HC		(2) CPP		(3) RC		(4) Real terms
Sales		25,000		25,000		25,000		25,000
Less expenses							
Cost of materials	10,000		12,000		15,000		15,000	
Wages	6,000		6,000		6,000		6,000	
Depreciation	2,400		2,880		3,600		3,600	
		18,400		20,880		24,600		24,600
Operating profit (loss)		6,600		4,120		400		400
Add holding gains (losses)							
Plant and machinery	–	–			6,000		3,600	
Stock	–	–			10,000		6,000	
Cash	–		(1000)		–		(1,000)	
				(1,000)		16,000		8,600
Total gains (losses)		£6,600		£3,120		£16,400		£9,000

Notes

Depreciation charges   HC: $1/5 \times £12,000 = £2,400$
                                    CPP: $1/5 (£12,000) \times 1.2) = £2,880$
          RC and RT: $1/5 \times £18,000 = £3,600$

Holding gain (losses)
    Plant and machinery   RC: $£18,000 - £12,000 = £6,000$
                                      RT: $£18,000 - (£12,000 \times 1.2) = £3,600$

Stock: RC: $£30,000 - £20,000 = £10,000$
        RT: $£30,000 - (£20,000 \times 1.2) = £6,000$

Cash: CPP and RT: $£5,000 - (£5,000 \times 1.2) = (£1,000)$

Balance sheets

	(1) HC	(2) CPP	(3) RC	(4) Real terms
Assets				
Plant (less depreciation)	9,600	11,520	14,400	14,400
Stock	25,000	27,000	30,000	30,000
Cash	9,000	9,000	9,000	9,000
	£43,600	£47,520	£53,400	£53,400
Financed by:				
Opening capital	37,000	37,000	37,000	37,000
Add capital maintenance adjustment	–	7,400	–	7,400
	£37,000	£44,400	£37,000	£44,400

Add total gains for year							
Holding gains	–		(1,000)		16,000		8,600
Operating profit	6,600		4,120		400		400
		6,600		3,120		16,400	9,000
		£43,600		£47,520		£53,400	£53,400

Notes

Closing cash balance: £5,000 − £6,000 (wages) + £25,000 (sale) − £15,000 (stock)

Plant values before depreciation	HC: £12,000
	CPP: £12,000 × 1.2 = £14,400
	RC and RT: £18,000

Stock values	HC: £10,000 + £15,000 = £25,000
	CPP: (£10,000 × 1.2) + £15,000 = £27,000
	RC and RT: £15,000 + £15,000 = £30,000

Capital maintenance adjustment: £37,000 × (1.2 − 1.0)

Note that under RC a capital maintenance adjustment of £16,000 (equal to the nominal holding gains on physical assets) would be made if it were intended to maintain physical capital.

Comment

The various profit figures show that the method of price change accounting can have a significant effect on reported profit, although the differences are amplified by the rather dramatic price changes assumed in the example.

If we are using operating profit as our profit measure, historical cost (HC) produces the largest profit in this case, followed fairly closely by constant purchasing power (CPP), with replacement cost (RC) and real terms (RT) lagging behind. This is because HC profit bears only the historical cost of materials and depreciation. CPP, on the other hand, bears these costs increased by a general index, and RC and RT both charge the costs at the current replacement price (which, in this example, has risen faster than the general price index). Thus HC operating profit can be said to include nominal holding gains on physical assets used (i.e., the difference between replacement cost at the time of use and money cost paid on acquisition). CPP operating profit includes only real holding gains (the difference between replacement cost and cost of acquisition adjusted by a general price index). RC and RT operating profit, on the other hand, charge replacement cost and so eliminate all holding gains on assets used up ('realised' holding gains).

If we look at holding gains, we obtain a very different picture. HC, by definition, reports no separate holding gains (although we have seen that realised holding gains are included in HC operating profit). CPP, by definition, shows no holding gains on physical assets (stock and plant) because these are assumed to increase by the general index, and cost adjusted by the general index is also the capital maintenance benchmark which we use in measuring gain or profit. However, CPP does show a holding *loss* on money, which has failed to rise in value to equal the capital maintenance benchmark. RC shows the largest holding gains, because it compares the current replacement costs of the physical assets with their historical money costs. RT also shows large holding gains on physical assets but these are lower than in the RC case because the capital maintenance benchmark is now indexed HC rather than money HC. Finally RT also reports a loss on holding money, the same as that in CPP, and for the same reason, i.e., the capital maintenance benchmark is adjusted by the general index.

The relative merits of the different measures depend on what qualities we are seeking. HC reports only *realised* profits, and it includes realised holding gains in operating profits. It makes no adjustment for the effects of general inflation on the measurement of capital. CPP does allow for the effect of inflation on capital and thus shows the loss on holding money, but it makes a somewhat artificial assumption that the cost of physical assets has moved in direct line with inflation. RC makes a strict separation between operating profit and holding gains on physical assets, and holding gains include unrealised gains (the difference between RC and HC of assets held at the end of the period). It does not make any allowance for the effects of general inflation, which might be thought to exaggerate the holding gains. RT remedies the latter deficiency: it calculates operating profit on a RC basis, but the holding gains are calculated after removing the effects of general inflation during the year. This adjustment for general inflation means that RT, like CPP, reports a loss on holding money.

In summary, HC has two possible deficiencies: it does not take account of general inflation or of changing prices of specific assets. CPP adapts HC to take account of the former (general inflation) and RC takes account of the latter (specific price changes). RT takes account of both. It should be noted that the distribution between realised and unrealised holding gains is sometimes thought to be important (because unrealised gains do not meet the realisation criterion). If this is the case, it might be better to report the unrealised gains (or losses) separately.

8 THE COLLECTION AND PROCESSING OF ACCOUNTING DATA

The Widget Wholesaling Company

(a)   Calculation of the correct amount of trade creditors

			£
Original total of list of balances			8,506
Add Item (1): Purchase not posted		52	
Item (3): Correction (reduction) of cash credited		54	
Item (6): Missing balance		64	
			170
Less Item (2): Wrong (second) posting of invoice		80	
Item (5): Wrong casting (reduce credit balance)		99	
			(179)
Correct balance			£8,497

Note that Item (4) is an error confined to the Day Book and does not affect the individual account balances, which we are correcting here.

(b)   *Calculation of correction to reported profit*

Corrections decreasing total purchases (as in the day book):

	£
Item (2): Elimination of wrong (second) record	80
Item (4): Correction of casting error	100
Total reduction of purchases	£180

None of the other items affects the total of the purchases day book. Hence, the corrections reduce purchases by £180 and increase profit by £180.

NOTES

I BASIC CONCEPTS

1 This is the point of the well-known balloon joke, much recited at accountants' dinners (and those of rival professions) which ends: 'How do you know I'm an accountant?' (Reply) 'Because your information is perfectly accurate and totally useless!'.

2 Provided, of course, an adequate recording system was in operation. Cash is the most liquid of assets and can flow rapidly in unforeseen directions, if not properly controlled and recorded.

3 The cash flows expected to arise from an asset are discounted by a rate of interest (or discount rate) to reduce them to a lower present value (PV) which reflects the amount which, if invested now, would accrue with interest to yield future amounts equal to the expected cash flows. In the discounted cash flow (DCF) method of investment appraisal the PV of a new investment is compared with cost. Investment is justified if PV is greater than or equal to cost.

2 THE ACCOUNTING FRAMEWORK

1 Goodwill is currently a controversial issue in accounting. The methods by which it is measured and recorded in practice bear little relationship to the concept described here.

2 Prudent accountants do not permit a mirror image provision for 'good creditors', i.e., those who never insist on payment.

3 An excellent advanced text book which summarises much of this evidence is George Foster, *Financial Statement Analysis* (Prentice Hall, 1986). This book is particularly strong in its discussion of the interpretation of financial statements.

4 Ian Griffiths' best-selling book on this subject (*Creative Accounting*, 1986) is recommended as an accessible and entertaining introduction.

3   THE ACCOUNTING SYSTEM: ELEMENTS OF DOUBLE
ENTRY ACCOUNTING

1 The reader who is familiar with computers will realise that example 3.1 could be generated by using a spread sheet system, which would make it less laborious to prepare. However, the accounting system which is developed subsequently (example 3.2) would still be more efficient and store more relevant information than the up-dated balance sheet and could equally well be implemented by using a computer.
2 In the next chapter, we shall take a more sophisticated view of this type of transaction, by splitting profit into its two basic components, sales and cost of sales.
3 This convention is violated by the British, but not by the American, method of presenting a horizontal format balance sheet.

4   THE ACCOUNTING SYSTEM: REVENUES AND EXPENSES

1 If the business were purely a trading concern, this would simply be called a trading account.
2 The peculiarities of company accounting practice in the UK mean that the appropriation section of the profit and loss account deals only with a limited part of shareholders' funds. Thus, whereas dividends (the company equivalent of drawings) are debited to the appropriation account, capital raised by issue of shares (the company version of capital introduced) is credited direct to the balance sheet. Various other gains, losses and adjustments (such as those resulting from revaluations of fixed assets) are also debited or credited direct to reserves (which are part of shareholders' funds) in the balance sheet, by-passing the profit and loss account. Such adjustments are a source of some of the creative accounting devices described in Ian Griffiths' *Creative Accounting*.
3 Another well-known intuitive conflict is that banks speak of 'crediting' the customer's account when money is paid in. The reason for this is that it is the bank which is keeping the account, and it is therefore recorded as a liability to the customer (a credit). From the customer's point of view, the bank account is an asset (a debit).

5   THE ACCOUNTING SYSTEM: ACCRUALS, PREPAYMENTS
AND DEPRECIATION

1 Note that accounting years do not have to coincide with calendar years, although 31 December is, in fact, a popular date on which to end the accounting year.
2 In general, substituting $C = £20,000$ and $D = £4,000$ into the equation, and rearranging terms, gives us $S = £20,000 - £4,000 \, L$.

3 This is derived as follows:

The written-down value of the asset (cost, less depreciation) at time L is $C(1-d)^L$.

We need to write down to scrap value, so that $S = C(1-d)^L$, which implies that

$$\sqrt[L]{\frac{S}{C}} = 1 - d$$

4 The allocation problem and the arbitrariness of methods of dealing with it in accounting generally has been most clearly exposed in two monographs by Arthur L. Thomas (*The Allocation Problem*, 1969, and *The Allocation Problem, Part II*, 1974, both published by the American Accounting Association), which any serious student of accounting theory should read.

5 A more advanced discussion of alternative valuation systems by the present author will be found in *Inflation Accounting, An Introduction to the Debate* (1983). A highly readable discussion of more advanced aspects of depreciation is Prof. W. T. Baxter's *Depreciation* (Sweet and Maxwell, 1971).

6 This name has obscure origins in the Accounting Department of the London School of Economics. The present author first heard it in Prof. William Baxter's introductory lectures in 1956. Prof. Baxter, an incurable optimist, pronounced the name 'right' rather than 'writhe'. The name also appears in elementary exercises used for many years in the Economics Department at Bristol, possibly taken there from LSE by Prof. David Solomons, who moved to Bristol in 1955.

7 Brackets are a conventional means of indicating negative balances in financial statements.

8 It would, in fact, be rather a poor return in this example, but the numerical examples in this book are designed to illustrate accounting technique rather than to be realistic.

9 In more sophisticated treatments, the 'add back' method may be superseded by techniques designed to show the total funds generated by operations, including working capital changes.

6 THE INTERPRETATION OF ACCOUNTS

1 Douglas Adams, *The Hitchhiker's Guide to the Galaxy*, Pan Books, 1979, p. 136.

2 Liquidation is the selling up of a company's assets to pay its debts when it becomes insolvent. Insolvency is inability to repay debts as and when they become due: it does not preclude the possibility of ultimate (delayed) repayment of all debts.

3 See, for example, the relevant sections of Ian Griffiths' *Creative Accounting*.

4 Risk is evaluated in the context of a portfolio of shares, i.e., variable returns may be very desirable, improving immunity from risk, if they vary inversely with the returns of other shares held. The principles of portfolio theory are explained in the book by Foster, *Financial Statement Analysis* and in any good introductory textbook on finance.

7 ACCOUNTING FOR PRICE CHANGES

1 We avoid here the well-known problems of defining a general index which will measure inflation in a satisfactory manner.

2 This illustration is used in the author's book, *Inflation Accounting, An Introduction to the Debate*, where it is developed much more fully.

3 Strictly, we need to assume that all the sales were made at the time when the replacement cost had risen to £1.25.

4 Strictly, we need to assume that all sales were made when the general price level was £110, otherwise it might be necessary to re-state sales in current prices, with other attendant complications.

5 These terms have their origins in the classic work of E. O. Edwards and P. W. Bell, *The Theory and Measurement of Business Income*, University of California Press, 1961.

6 This would have the same effect on profit as the historical cost treatment, in which the realised holding gain is effectively deducted from the cost of sales (by charging historical rather than current cost).

7 We have already seen that the determination of the rate of depreciation is not a trivial matter. In certain methods of current value accounting, it is possible to avoid the problem of determining a depreciation rate by, instead, revaluing the asset at the end of each accounting period, thus allowing periodic depreciation (or appreciation) to be determined by reference to the market.

8 In a more realistic example, in which the asset had been held over previous periods, there would also be an adjustment for 'backlog' depreciation. This would be debited to accumulated depreciation and credited to the revaluation reserve.

9 The relevant period is the whole accounting period for assets held at the beginning of the period, and the period since acquisition date for those assets acquired during the accounting period.

10 Such a measure was proposed in 1975 in the United Kingdom by the Sandilands Report, the report of a government-appointed committee.

11 They are discussed in detail by the present author in *Inflation Accounting, An Introduction to the Debate*, Cambridge University Press, 1983.

8 THE COLLECTION AND PROCESSING OF ACCOUNTING DATA

1 Alternative terms are 'personal' instead of 'subordinate' and 'purchases' rather than 'trade creditors'.

2 Another common form of discount is a 'trade discount' which does not depend upon prompt payment and is therefore effectively merely a price reduction at the time of sale.

3 The corresponding credits are to discounts received (an income account which is transferred to profit and loss at the end of the period) and to cash (a reduction in the total cash balance in the balance sheet).

9 SOME EXTENSIONS AND SUGGESTIONS FOR FURTHER READING

1 The description derives from the fact that the residual profits of equity shareholders are made more volatile (i.e., 'geared' or 'levered' up) by the fact that the fixed claim element (loan stock and preferred stock) takes a fixed slice out of profits.

2 In particular in 'Financial Accounting Theory: An Overview', *The British Accounting Review*, Autumn 1986, pp. 4–41, which gives a much more extensive treatment of the issues which are touched upon here.

3 Before natural scientists are allowed to mock this, they should be reminded that Newton was one of many who looked for the philosopher's stone (which would turn base metals to gold). If he had studied economics instead, he would have realised that in the likely event that such a technology could not be kept secret, the effect of the discovery would be to drive down the price of gold.

4 These are the so-called dual values, which represent the opportunity cost of the resources which are in short supply.

5 H. T. Johnson and R. S. Kaplan, *Relevance Lost: The Rise and Fall of Management Accounting*, Boston, 1987.

6 This book is at present out of print.

INDEX

Lightning Source UK Ltd.
Milton Keynes UK
UKOW041151081112

201860UK00001B/46/A